THE ROMANTIC ASSERTION

THE ROMANTIC ASSERTION

*A Study in the Language
of Nineteenth Century Poetry*

by

R. A. FOAKES

BARNES & NOBLE, Inc.
New York
METHUEN & CO. Ltd
London

First published, 1958

This edition reprinted, 1971
by Barnes & Noble, Inc.
and Methuen & Co. Ltd.

Barnes & Noble ISBN 389 04147 5

Methuen ISBN 416 60710 1

Printed in the United States of America

CONTENTS

PREFACE   page 7

1 THE COMMITMENT TO METAPHOR   11
  Modern criticism and Romantic poetry

2 POETIC IMAGERY   23

3 ORDER OUT OF CHAOS   39
  The task of the Romantic poet

4 THE UNFINISHED JOURNEY   51
  Wordsworth's *The Prelude*

5 THE VISION OF LOVE   80
  Keats's *The Eve of St. Agnes* and Shelley's *Adonais*

6 THE RHETORIC OF FAITH   111
  Tennyson's *In Memoriam* and Browning's *Men and Women*

7 THE VANITY OF RHETORIC   149
  Matthew Arnold's poetry and James Thomson's *The City of Dreadful Night*

CONCLUSION   181

INDEX   183

PREFACE

THIS essay starts from the preoccupation of many modern critics with metaphor, and their consequent dislike or avoidance of much nineteenth-century poetry, which has little metaphor (in the common sense of the term). In it I have tried to examine the way in which language is used in this poetry, tracing in particular the development of two structural images, which I have called the journey of life and the vision of love, and the association of these with a vocabulary of value-words in some major poems or groups of poems. It is not an exhaustive survey, but an exploratory study, which concentrates attention on some neglected aspects of this poetry, and may, I hope, be of help to students and others who do not easily respond to it.

In outlining and discussing certain critical attitudes in the first two chapters, I have not attempted to do justice to the achievement and scope of modern criticism, or to the work of individual critics mentioned, but have simplified in order to bring out what seems relevant to the study of Romantic poetry, and in particular to emphasize how much we are hampered by critical preconceptions derived from the poetry of our own age from giving nineteenth-century poetry the attention due to it. The rest of this book will perhaps show how much I have learned from the critics cited at the beginning; in particular I am indebted to M. H. Abrams, *The Mirror and the Lamp*, and to W. K. Wimsatt Jr., *The Verbal Icon*.

A large part of this book was drafted while I was a visitor as a Commonwealth Fund Fellow at Yale University, and my work was much aided by the hospitality and kindness of the Master and Fellows of Davenport College. I am most grateful to Professor Cleanth Brooks, Professor Maynard Mack, and Mr R. J. Dorius for help, advice and criticism. This book

PREFACE

of course in no way reflects their views, any more than it does those of many others who have assisted me, among whom my thanks go especially to Professor Clifford Leech for many wise comments and suggestions, to Professor E. A. Horsman, Mr N. S. Brooke, and to my wife.

R. A. FOAKES

Durham
May 1957

Idly talk they who speak of poets as mere indulgers of fancy, imagination, superstition, etc., They are the bridlers by delight, the purifiers; they that combine all these with reason and order—the true protoplasts who tame the chaos.

S. T. COLERIDGE, *Anima Poetae*

[1]
THE COMMITMENT TO METAPHOR
Modern Criticism and Romantic Poetry

I

Two recent books[1] have demonstrated to what extent modern poetry and the most influential modern criticism are indebted to the Romantic tradition in spite of a frequently proclaimed antipathy to Romantic attitudes. In his penetrating study of the continuance of this tradition, Frank Kermode would place T. E. Hulme, W. B. Yeats, Ezra Pound and others fully in it; he says of Hulme's concept of the 'intensive manifold',

> it is accessible only to intuition, belonging to a different order of reality. It is 'indescribable but not unknowable'. The artist knows it; it is his Image. It is finite; hence the need for precision. Its meaning is the same thing as its form, and the artist is absolved from participation with the discursive powers of the intellect.
>
> This theory, as Hulme explains it, makes a show of being in opposition to Romantic imprecision . . . but in fact it is fundamentally a new statement of the old defence of poetry against positivism and the universe of death. It is a revised form of the old proclamation that poetry has special access to truth, and is not merely light entertainment for minds tired out by physics.[2]

This is acutely perceived, but if it is incorrect to see modern criticism simply as a reaction against Romanticism, it is equally an oversimplification to treat Hulme's attacks on

---

[1] John Bayley, *The Romantic Survival* and Frank Kermode, *Romantic Image*, both published in 1957: these appeared after this study was drafted, but the first chapter has since been rewritten. [2] *Romantic Image*, p. 129.

humanism, romanticism and imprecision as of little significance. What seems rather to be displayed by Hulme and to have persisted in the work of later critics is a confusion of attitudes which are in many ways contradictory. This may be brought out sufficiently for the scope of the present study by reference to remarks by two important modern critics.

In his essays on *Tradition and the Individual Talent* (1917) and *The Function of Criticism* (1923), T. S. Eliot said that the critic works to correct taste by setting a new poet 'for contrast and comparison among the dead'. He attacked 'interpretation' as illegitimate, without defining exactly what this word meant to him, and argued that no poet has his complete meaning alone, but only in relation to the 'simultaneous order' composed by all literature. In general, the attitude outlined in these essays is an objective one, corresponding to what Mr Eliot called classicism, the need for men to give allegiance to something, an unquestioned spiritual authority, outside themselves. For immediate purposes, the classical outlook may be described in terms of an assumption that there is an order which provides a frame of reference for evaluating all things. In general terms, this order may be represented in myths, in religions, in a social order, in the great chain of being; art partaking of such an order finds its subject-matter in the possibilities or failures of life in the context of the order, and as it has a common frame of reference, it tends to make use of common forms and observe classical rules. The function of criticism in relation to such art is of an objective kind, in that works of art may be judged in terms of one another and in relation to the common frame of reference; they compose a simultaneous order.

W. K. Wimsatt, Junior, in his *The Verbal Icon* (1954), observes how Mr Eliot praised an objective attitude in criticism, described fact-finding as a valuable activity, and attacked as corrupters of taste 'those who supply opinion or fancy', but points out that much of Mr Eliot's own criticism consists of exhortations, opinions and judgements of a per-

MODERN CRITICISM AND ROMANTIC POETRY

sonal kind. There is a discrepancy between his theory and his practice, and in his practice he seems to fall into what Mr Wimsatt calls the 'affective fallacy', reporting his feelings in an impressionistic way, describing what a poem does rather than what it is. Mr Wimsatt also complains of criticism which falls into the 'intentional fallacy', or commences from the author's intentions, and defines the critic's function thus:

> The function of the objective critic is by approximate descriptions of poems, or multiple restatements of their meaning, to aid other readers to come to an intuitive and full realization of poems themselves, and hence to know good poems and distinguish them from bad ones.[1]

This is an interesting definition because the word 'objective' seems to be at odds with what the critic is supposed to do. It would seem that he is to regard the poem as unique, existing in and for itself, as autotelic, a line of thought which can be traced back to Romantic theories of art as organic; he is to analyse a poem's meaning by practical criticism, and to judge it presumably in terms of complexity and integration. Except for its special emphasis on meaning, this mode of criticism is in fact a subjective one, and stems from a Romantic outlook. By this is meant the assumption that there is no general order, that in an anarchic society in which men are isolated from one another, a principle of order must be sought within the self. It is in this sense that Romantic poetry is subjective, in that the poet creates his own order; there are no formal rules for him to work by, and he is likely to be praised for originality. The criticism appropriate for such poetry is subjective, the kind of criticism that Mr Eliot

---

[1] *The Verbal Icon*, p. 83. I am deliberately abstracting from a subtle and complicated discussion by W. K. Wimsatt, but I hope not unfairly. Several of his penetrating essays in this volume are concerned with the nature and limitations of modern criticism, but while he clearly recognizes that Romantic poetry works in a different way from metaphysical and modern poetry, and has a different structure, he tries to accommodate it within the terms of modern criticism, metaphor, wit, complexity, etc.

objected to so strongly and practised, as Mr Wimsatt noticed, so consistently, and the kind of criticism defined by Mr Wimsatt as 'objective'.

In the senses of the terms outlined above, it might be said that in spite of his advocation of a classical attitude, Mr Eliot writes criticism which belongs to the Romantic tradition; and that Mr Wimsatt, for all that he accepts fully the Romantic view that 'A poem should not mean but be', and proposes a subjective reading of each poem as a contained whole, wishes to claim a classical or objective character for such criticism. The combination of opposed attitudes represented in these critics is very common in modern criticism, which, like criticism at any period, is closely linked to what poets are trying to do, to the evaluation and defence of contemporary poetry. This may be seen in the attempts that have been made in the last forty years to describe new poetry in Mr Eliot's terms as a modification of an already established order of the past, to exercise a classical function and place modern poetry in relation to a supposedly objective order. This has involved much rewriting of literary history. As Frank Kermode has brilliantly shown in his examination of T. S. Eliot's concept of a 'dissociation of sensibility' taking place in the seventeenth century, and its counterparts in the views of other critics like T. E. Hulme and W. B. Yeats, this has consisted of a search for a

> golden age when the prevalent mode of knowing was not positivist and anti-imaginative; when the Image, the intuited, creative reality was habitually respected; when art was not permanently on the defensive against mechanical and systematic modes of inquiry. Since the order of reality postulated as the proper study of the poet tends, in one way or another, to be granted supernatural attributes, the ideal epoch is usually a religious one.[1]

In particular, there has been a widespread upgrading of early seventeenth-century poetry, including Jacobean tragedy, and

---

[1] *Romantic Image*, p. 148.

MODERN CRITICISM AND ROMANTIC POETRY

a devaluation of Milton and of much Romantic and nineteenth-century poetry. Both the combination of Romantic and classical attitudes in modern criticism, and the tendency to depreciate or disregard the poetry of the nineteenth century, and incidentally long poems in general, point to important differences between the poetry of the present age and Romantic poetry. Our world is still the world of the Romantics in so far as it seems anarchic, as the poet needs to impose an order on the chaos of existence; but it differs from theirs in significant respects, for instance in the growth of an urban way of life[1] in which the breakdown of ties, the isolation of the individual in the crowd, has become notorious; in the decay of faith in the face of material and scientific advances which appear to have taken control of man's destiny; in a shift from optimism about man's possible greatness to despair of his ever achieving a harmonious world. The predominant note of Romantic poetry is its assertion, its vision of a universe or a society resolved into concord, of 'the one life within us and abroad', of

> *The feeling of life endless, the great thought*
> *By which we live, Infinity and God,*
>
> (Wordsworth, *The Prelude*, XIII.183-4)

or of man as 'Sceptreless, free, uncircumscribed ... the King Over himself; just, gentle, wise'. The predominant note of modern poetry is its sense of conflict or tension; the poets no longer offer general solutions, only local and particular ones, and the universal vision has given way to images of disintegration or local and personal resolutions of conflicts, the sense that 'I can connect Nothing with nothing', the image of 'That dolphin-torn, that gong-tormented sea', the defiance of joy to set against despair,

[1] Wordsworth could hardly have foreseen the overwhelming urbanization of modern life when he complained at the beginning of the century of the 'increasing accumulation of men in cities', which he saw as one of a number of forces then combining to blunt 'the discriminating powers of the mind' (*Preface to Lyrical Ballads*, 1800); but the process had commenced then.

THE COMMITMENT TO METAPHOR

*Some moralist or mythological poet
Compares the soul to a solitary swan;
I am satisfied with that,
Satisfied if a troubled mirror show it,
Before that brief gleam of its life be gone,
An image of its state;
The wings half spread for flight,
The breast thrust out in pride
Whether to play, or to ride
Those winds that clamour of approaching night.*

(W. B. Yeats, *Nineteen Hundred and Nineteen*)

The cross-breeding of Romantic and classical attitudes in criticism is connected with this change in poetry from a vision of universal order to a reflection of disintegration or images of local order. The mirroring of disintegration in, for instance T. S. Eliot's *The Waste Land*, is given shape and strength in terms of the order and magnificence of past ages and literatures of the past; and the local images of order in, for instance, the poetry of W. B. Yeats, are given validity in the context of Byzantium, Urbino or Coole Park. Modern poets tend to look for a historical period which seems to reflect the qualities they value,[1] in order to establish their local images and personal resolutions of oppositions as being of general significance, to create for them the context of a larger frame of reference. The transcendental vision of the Romantic poet, which makes use of 'the kind of symbol which is rooted in our universal natural experience', gives place to a limited vision disturbed by an overriding sense of disorder, which tends to employ personal images that have to be 'validated by the manipulation of the artist in a special context'.[2] One result of this change is that modern criticism gives special attention to the study of poetic imagery in the narrow sense of metaphor and simile, that, as Mr Wimsatt says, 'The theorist of poetry tends more and more today to make metaphor the irreducible

---

[1] See Frank Kermode, *Romantic Image*, p. 145.
[2] These phrases are borrowed from Robert Penn Warren, *The Rime of the Ancient Mariner* (New York, 1946), p. 75.

element of his definition of poetry.'[1] The transcendental vision has diminished into the image, into metaphor.

II

The growth of interest in poetic imagery can be related to the development of organic theories of art in the nineteenth century. The notion of the unconscious mind became useful to account for poetry valued as being unpremeditated, the spontaneous overflow of powerful feelings, so that Carlyle could assert, 'unconsciousness is the sign of creation'.[2] Poetry came to be regarded as non-propositional, as expressing feeling and being independent of truth, and hence as having an intrinsic value as an end in itself. In this way critics were able to combat the seeming encroachment of science upon all aspects of life and the world, what some felt to be a circumscribing of the imagination, by distinguishing between scientific truth and poetic truth. The finest poetry was identified with the most impassioned language, and the lyric or short poem took on a special character as 'more eminently and peculiarly poetry than any other'.[3]

Such views underlie the modern concern with poetic imagery. The work of the unconscious mind has come to be associated particularly with metaphor and simile, and the assumption is often made that there is some kind of borderline in poetry between 'conscious' reference and 'unconscious' image, the latter being the more valuable. The most impassioned language and the most imaginative language are thought to coalesce in metaphor, which is regarded as the supreme mode of expression, the true essence of poetry; and a commonplace nineteenth-century distinction between poetry as expressing feeling and prose as conveying information, rephrased now in the assertion that poetry employs

[1] *The Verbal Icon*, p. 128.
[2] *Characteristics* (1831), cited in M. H. Abrams, *The Mirror and the Lamp* (New York, 1953), p. 217; this contains an excellent full account of the development of the ideas touched on here.
[3] Cited from *Early Essays by John Stuart Mill*, edited J. W. M. Gibbs (1897), p. 208, in Abrams, *The Mirror and the Lamp*, p. 98.

THE COMMITMENT TO METAPHOR

the connotations (associations) of words as well as the denotations, prose only the denotations (the literal senses), is extended to embrace imagery: 'The imagery of poetry is in the main complex and suggestive; the imagery of prose single and explicit.'[1] A regard for metaphor as the essence of poetry encouraged the analysis of poetic imagery for its own sake, and often in isolation from its context, so that the poem tends to disappear as the image takes its place. Some critics make a further distinction in value between the terms of the image, considering the vehicle (subject-matter)[2] as of special importance as welling up from the poet's unconscious mind, in contrast to the tenor (object-matter or reference) which is ignored as having merely, as it were, a prose character.

These are some ways in which the present interest in imagery may be seen as allied to the organic theories of poetry which developed with the Romantic movement; but at the same time this interest reflects a kind of poetry and a kind of criticism which differ greatly from Romantic poetry and Romantic criticism, and are in large measure hostile to them. The differences are most clearly seen in the criticism which has been influenced by the ideas of T. S. Eliot, T. E. Hulme and I. A. Richards. The last-named developed a psychological theory of the value of poetry, which, like nineteenth-century critics, he claimed was independent of scientific truth, and he argued that critical study should be devoted to the evaluation of a poem as an end in itself:

> Every poem . . . is a strictly limited piece of experience, a piece which breaks up more or less easily if alien elements intrude.

[1] Middleton Murry, 'Metaphor', in *Shakespeare Criticism, 1919-1935*, edited Ann Bradby (1936), p. 234.

[2] I. A. Richards in *The Philosophy of Rhetoric* (New York, 1936) called the term imported to illustrate or modify the underlying idea in an image the 'vehicle' (which is the same as the 'subject-matter' of Caroline Spurgeon, *Shakespeare's Imagery and what it tells us*, 1935, and the 'minor term' of H. W. Wells, *Poetic Imagery*, New York, 1924); the other term becomes the 'tenor' (or 'object-matter', though Miss Spurgeon did not use this word, or 'major term'). These terms have also been called 'content' and 'reference' by Owen Barfield, *Poetic Diction* (1928).

MODERN CRITICISM AND ROMANTIC POETRY
We must keep the poem undisturbed by these or we fail to read it and have some other experience instead. For these reasons we establish a severance; we draw a boundary between the poem and what is not the poem in our experience.[1]

Good poetry became 'inclusive' poetry, which offered an experience in its entirety, complex and full of contradictions, and this was contrasted with 'exclusive' poetry, which omitted unpleasant or discordant impulses. The Romantic resolution of all things into a general harmony was thus altered and reduced to a resolution of the contradictions within a 'strictly limited piece of experience'; and the best poems, which are self-sustaining, are those which reconcile oppositions in this limited sense, and emerge into irony or paradox.

The poem then becomes a 'pattern of resolved stresses',[2] built out of conflict. The 'affective fallacy' and the 'intentional fallacy' are denounced because 'The outcome of either fallacy ... is that the poem itself, as an object of specifically critical judgement, tends to disappear.'[3] The greatness of a poet 'depends upon the extent of the area of experience which he can master poetically', and 'inclusiveness' is the mark of the good poet, who

> proves his vision by submitting it to the fires of irony, ... wishes to indicate that his vision has been earned, that it can survive reference to the complexities and contradictions of experience.[4]

Three terms in particular have come into use as measures for analysing and judging poems, all arising from the idea that a good poem must 'work by contradiction and qualification' in order to display the conflicting elements which, it is assumed, are characteristic of experience: the only solution for the poet, it has been claimed, is paradox, and the language of poetry

[1] *The Principles of Literary Criticism* (1924), p. 78.
[2] Cleanth Brooks, *The Well Wrought Urn* (New York, 1947), p. 186.
[3] *The Verbal Icon*, p. 21.
[4] Robert Penn Warren, 'Pure and Impure Poetry', *Kenyon Review*, V (1943), 250, 252.

THE COMMITMENT TO METAPHOR

has been identified with 'The Language of Paradox'.[1] This first term, paradox, suggesting a strict opposition of meanings, has perhaps seemed to many critics too rigid a schematization to be applied to poetry, and the word 'tension' has been used to indicate something of the same idea, that in good poetry there must be a tension between opposing themes. It has been given a special sense in relation to the philosophical terms 'extension' and 'intension': 'the meaning of poetry is its "tension", the full organized body of the extension and intension that we can find in it', that is, of the literal and figurative significances.[2] The third term, irony, is related to the other two, inasmuch as the poetry of paradox, of tension, is 'able to fuse the irrelevant and discordant, has come to terms with itself, and is invulnerable to irony'; hence irony becomes a 'principle of structure' in good poetry.[3]

The development and application of these terms has been fortified also by the reaction against humanism and romanticism, the demand for a poetry 'all dry and hard', finite and precise, stimulated by T. E. Hulme.[4] The poetry of T. S. Eliot was acclaimed as the first to employ techniques 'adequate to the ways of feeling or modes of thought of adult sensitive moderns', to break away from a sterile Victorian tradition which saw 'the actual world as alien, recalcitrant and unpoetical'.[5] The new poetry and the new criticism were related to seventeenth-century poetry, and other literature has come to be measured against these as representing 'the consciousness of the age'.[6] Three of the criteria used in judging poetry in this way are especially significant. One is the treatment of all poetry as if it were contemporary poetry, which can be detached from its context in time and studied

---

[1] *The Well Wrought Urn*, Chapter 1; the quotation is on p. 9.
[2] Allen Tate, 'Tension in Poetry' (1938), in *On the Limits of Poetry. Selected Essays: 1928-48* (New York, 1948), p. 83.
[3] Cleanth Brooks, 'Irony as a Principle of Structure', in *Literary Opinion in America*, edited Morton D. Zabel (Revised Edition, New York, 1951), p. 732.
[4] *Speculations* (1924), p. 126.
[5] F. R. Leavis, *New Bearings in English Poetry* (1932), pp. 25, 15.
[6] F. R. Leavis writing in *Scrutiny*, II (1932), 134-5.

MODERN CRITICISM AND ROMANTIC POETRY

without reference to its historical meanings. Another is the demand for complexity, for the inclusion of the 'extraneous and distracting elements which might seem to contradict what the poet wishes to communicate'[1]; this kind of complexity, consisting in the balance and tension between conflicting elements held in suspension in the unity of the poem and emerging in irony and paradox, is characteristic of metaphysical and much modern poetry, and is perhaps only possible in a relatively short poem. A third criterion is the demand that each line of a poem be able to bear the severest scrutiny, that each line reflect the qualities of 'inclusive' poetry.

The long poem does not fulfil this kind of demand ('The apology of a long poem should be: "I am really a long *short poem*" '[2]), and is not amenable to the methods of analysis which have developed in association with the new critical standards, methods which seek to identify closely the possibilities of meaning in each line of 'inclusive' poetry, as these range from simple ambiguity to a full contradiction of opposed meanings. The most vivid and characteristic means by which the tension of opposed meanings is sustained within the line or short poem is metaphor, and consequently metaphor takes chief place in the study of poetry, 'the metaphysicals and the modernists stand opposed to the neoclassic and Romantic poets on the issue of metaphor'.[3]

What the critic looks for in a poem is a structure of meanings contained largely in its metaphor, and forming an autonomous whole to be evaluated in and for itself. Although such a view stems from a Romantic theory of poetry, for instance in its claim that poetry is autotelic, an end in itself, it represents an outlook that is generally hostile or indifferent to Romantic and Victorian poetry. It parades the old idea, deriving from Mallarmé and the earlier conception of a poem

[1] Cleanth Brooks, *The Well Wrought Urn*, p. 46.
[2] Laura Riding and Robert Graves, *A Survey of Modernist Poetry* (1927), p. 57.
[3] Cleanth Brooks, *Modern Poetry and the Tradition* (Chapel Hill, 1939), p. 22.

THE COMMITMENT TO METAPHOR

as a spontaneous product of feeling, that a poem should not mean but be, but twists this into a new significance by then asserting that a poem can only be through its meaning.[1] It uses formulae derived from Coleridge, seeing the poem also as a product of imagination, but it modifies the character of the imagination so that it merges into intelligence.[2] It has substituted for the Romantic idea of a poem as revealing eternal verities, the concept of a complex of limited meanings; a poet is more likely to be castigated for being unintelligent than for lacking imagination, to be disapproved for failing to exploit the full resources of words than for having nothing urgent to say. The Romantic commitment to a vision has given way to a narrower, more intellectual poetry, in which the only commitment is a commitment to metaphor: 'One can sum up modern poetic technique by calling it the rediscovery of metaphor and the full commitment to metaphor.'[3]

The technique of much modern criticism could be summed up in the same terms. Some of the critics who share this outlook like to think that the language of Romantic and Victorian poetry is shown to be inadequate by its failure to measure up to their criticism; but it seems better to suppose that their criticism is unsuitable for this kind of poetry, that what is called carelessness, a lack of intelligence, or a failure to represent the conflicting elements of experience, may be 'more often the highly adroit and skilful writing of a kind of poetry which they do not understand because they do not like that kind of poetry'.[4] The following chapters seek to explore tentatively the ways in which the language of this poetry works, poetry that is not committed to metaphor.

[1] *The Verbal Icon*, p. 4.
[2] So for instance F. R. Leavis says of Milton that his 'defect of intelligence is a defect of imagination', *Revaluation*, p. 58.
[3] Cleanth Brooks, 'Irony as a Principle of Structure', p. 729.
[4] F. A. Pottle, 'The Case of Shelley', *PMLA*, LXVII (1952), 605.

[2]

POETIC IMAGERY

THE oppositions so frequently set up between prose and poetry, scientific and emotive language, poetic and prosaic thought, poetic and prosaic imagery, are valid to a certain degree. It is generally agreed that poetry is the most intense and imaginative form of literary expression. At the same time, no absolute divisions can be made; much verse is unimaginative, much prose highly imaginative. It would seem rather that there is a slow gradation from the highest poetic flight down to the abstract symbols of science, and only these last are perhaps completely lacking in the power to evoke feelings and thoughts beyond their literal meaning. The concentration of attention on poetic imagery, however, coincides with the further assumptions that metaphor is central in poetry and embodies an author's imaginative vision, and, frequently, that only the subject-matter (vehicle) of the imagery in a poem is really important, as welling up from the unconscious mind, which is conceived as the mainspring of the imagination. Those critics who regard paradox, irony and the inclusion of all the discordant elements of an experience as essential to poetry, are inclined to reject simile:

> Simile, like prose, is analytic, metaphor, like poetry, is synthetic; simile is extensive, metaphor intensive; simile is logical and judicious, metaphor illogical and dogmatic; simile reasons, metaphor apprehends by intuition . . . simile is to metaphor as prose is to poetry.[1]

They are also inclined to reject all poetry in which metaphor plays a small part as sentimental or simply bad: the poetry of

[1] W. B. Stanford, *Greek Metaphor* (Oxford, 1936), pp. 28-29.

the Romantic period is severely attacked, that of the nineteenth century virtually ignored.

Already in his *The Symbolist Movement in Literature* (1899) which influenced Yeats and T. S. Eliot, Arthur Symons adumbrated such a view in his praise of symbolism as

> an attempt to spiritualize literature, to evade the old bondage of rhetoric, the old bondage of exteriority. Description is banished that beautiful things may be evoked, magically: the regular beat of verse is broken in order that words may fly.[1]

By rhetoric he seems to have meant the use of words and images as counters intended to rouse feelings rather than to make the reader see an object; he pronounced the judgement, 'All art hates the vague; not the mysterious, but the vague.'[2] All that poetry which depends for much of its strength on rhetoric in this sense, on a direct appeal to feelings through words or images which evoke stock responses, and on vagueness as an attribute of the aspiration which it often seeks to communicate, was dismissed: it has become a widely accepted view that

> The point to make about Romantic poetry now is not the one about its noble words, but a negative and nasty one: the noble words are almost absurdly incoherent.[3]

This poetry gains its effect not through metaphor, but by means of rhetoric, incantation, sweeping rhythms, repetition (as in the ballad, a form characteristically brought back into circulation by the Romantic movement), or by presenting, as Maud Bodkin might have called it,[4] a vivid embodiment of an enduring myth; by realizing again in a new form the power which an old and well-known story may have to offer some kind of allegory of man's life. Epic and narrative poetry are

---

[1] *The Symbolist Movement in Literature*, p. 9.
[2] Ibid., p. 153.
[3] J. C. Ransom, *The New Criticism* (Norfolk, Conn., 1941), p. 306.
[4] See her *Archetypal Patterns in Poetry* (1934).

POETIC IMAGERY

not usually amenable to analysis by metaphor,[1] and like Romantic poetry tend to employ evocative description rather than metaphor. Poetic imagery in its usual sense need not be used to embody the poet's vision, and may not be essential to poetry, at least to all kinds of poetry. It has become central in criticism only in the last fifty years, when a dislocation of values so affects the poets that they can no longer rely on an audience with a shared outlook; when they complain, 'you must create the meaning of each poem out of your private experience'[2]; when a habit of allusion and irony is adopted and the affirmation of values avoided; when the meaning of life is uncertain and long poems are unnecessary, so that the pronouncement of Symons, after Poe, becomes almost dogma, 'No long poem was ever written.'[3]

Definitions of poetic imagery, or of metaphor, have usually been made in relation to modern poetry, the poetry of Donne and the metaphysicals, or the poetry of Shakespeare and the Jacobean dramatists, and also in relation to the purpose of the critic. The name 'poetic image' is misleading as having no real relation to metaphor; it suggests one common way of thinking about metaphor, as a 'picture made out of words'.[4] This definition, which is basic to critics like Miss Spurgeon who are interested in an author's pictorial imagination, does not distinguish metaphor from simple description, which may equally well evoke a mental picture. It is inadequate not only because it is not specific, but because it is too limited, for a poetic image may have little or no sensory appeal, and visualization by the reader may be irrelevant or absurd.[5]

[1] As W. B. Stanford ound, when, after proclaiming that metaphor is central in poetry, and dismissing even simile as prosaic, he left himself nothing to say about the *Odyssey* and the *Iliad*; the final chapters of his *Greek Metaphor* are devoted to explaining why there is hardly any metaphor in Homer.

[2] Cecil Day Lewis, *A Hope for Poetry* (1934), p. 29.

[3] Op. cit., p. 137.

[4] Cecil Day Lewis, *The Poetic Image* (1947), p. 18.

[5] This is true, for instance, of much of the 'radical' imagery of the metaphysical poets, which depends for its effect on 'making psychological action clear by expressing it in terms of physical action'; see Alice S. Brandenburg, 'The Dynamic Image in Metaphysical Poetry', *PMLA*, LVII (1942), 1041.

Another fairly common definition of metaphor is best stated in the words of S. J. Brown: 'in its most characteristic and distinctive form it is the using of material objects as images of immaterial, spiritual things'.[1] This idea, more familiarly but less satisfactorily expressed as the presentation of the abstract through the concrete, would include much poetry that is not commonly regarded as metaphorical; it would include what has been called symbolic description, the power much narrative or simple description has of suggesting a spiritual condition, of being a kind of sustained vehicle or subject-matter, as for example the narrative of *The Rime of the Ancient Mariner*. In addition, a 'material object', a concrete image, is not necessary to metaphor; it may be merely implied, or it may not be present at all.

A third way of defining a poetic image is that derived from Aristotle, as a perception of hidden analogies, or 'the intuitive perception of similarity in dissimilarities'.[2] This again does not seem adequate: the perception of analogy, however widely dissimilar the objects or ideas concerned, does not make a poetic image. There is nothing figurative in the expressions 'That house is as high as a telegraph pole', or 'a grass-green coat'; both are literal evaluations.[3] To say 'That house is as high as heaven' does, however, constitute a figurative expression, but not because of any analogy between the terms. The first two phrases convey an exact image and the analogy is the important factor in understanding them, whereas the third conveys merely a vague image, if any, and what analogy there is seems unimportant. The first two give information, the last intensifies the quality of the house, tells

[1] *The World of Imagery* (1927), pp. 17-18.
[2] J. Middleton Murry, 'Metaphor', in Anne Bradby (Editor), *Shakespeare Criticism, 1919-1935*, p. 228.
[3] The distinction between a simple comparison as non-figurative, and a simile as intensifying a 'quality or action to an indefinite high degree' was observed by T. Hilding Svartengren in his *Intensifying Similes in English* (Lund, Sweden, 1918), p. xxii. Some apparently literal comparisons may be endowed with this intensifying quality by the force of a particular context, and the borderline between the literal and the figurative is not, of course, as clear as, for the immediate purposes of the argument, it is assumed to be here.

us about the feelings of the person looking at it, makes us experience it in a new way.

The best functional definition of metaphor, that of W. B. Stanford,[1] is derived from the Aristotelian view:

> The term metaphor is fully valid only when applied to a very definite and a rather complicated concept, viz. the process and result of using a term (X) normally signifying an object or concept (A) in such a context that it must refer to another object or concept (B) which is distinct enough in characteristics from (A) to ensure that in the composite idea formed by the syntheses of the concepts A and B and now symbolized in the word X, the factors A and B retain their conceptual independence even while they merge in the unity symbolized by X.

This is a precise and clear statement, but it omits what is perhaps the characteristic feature of metaphor, its intensification or redeployment of feeling. The function of metaphor is not simply to make us understand a 'composite idea', but rather to enable us to evaluate and to appreciate through a full perception the experience with which it deals. It is questionable whether metaphor creates a unity of concept often or at all; the unity it establishes seems often to be one of feeling or attitude, brought about through the conjunction of the general contexts of meaning and association of the two terms. So it would be difficult to say what composite idea emerges from the familiar image,

Sleep that knits up the ravell'd sleave of care.

The clash of contexts forces into prominence those elements of meaning and association which mutually support one another in the two terms, so that the indication of the process of mending, restoring what is torn or disjointed, in 'knits up the ravell'd sleave of care', directs our feeling towards the beneficial aspects of sleep; and the tension between the terms

[1] *Greek Metaphor* (Oxford, 1936), p. 101.

POETIC IMAGERY

is resolved in a heightened sense of the healing quality of sleep. This image indicates another aspect of metaphor neglected in W. B. Stanford's definition, namely, that the two terms are not usually of equivalent value. One is likely to be rooted in the immediate context of the play or poem, the tenor (object-matter) in this case being 'sleep', and the function of the other term, the vehicle (subject-matter), is commonly to qualify it in some way. The vehicle, in this case the 'ravell'd sleave', may have an independent life through its relationship to a larger pattern of imagery in the whole work, in this instance, perhaps clothing.

It would probably be easy to criticize any definition of poetic imagery which is made as a practical definition, for a very long analysis would be required to account for every feature of its working. All the definitions of the poetic image, of metaphor, which have been discussed, as a word-picture, as the perception of hidden analogy, as the presentation of the spiritual through a concrete image, as the creation of a composite idea, a unity of two terms which still remain independent, have a measure of truth; but they were selected by the various critics who use them as tools with which to discuss poetry, and are to that extent directed towards special ends. The attempt at a further definition which follows is made not in the hope that it will be more profound or adequate than these others, but in order to direct attention to a kind of poetry which they, on the whole, ignore.

Some of the main characteristics of metaphor and simile need to be noted first. In the poetic image two or more ideas are brought into relationship; one is the basic idea underlying the image, the other a term imported, or substituted for the literal statement of what is meant, which illuminates or modifies emotionally the basic idea, so that in some sense the bringing of the two terms together creates a unity in which they both share. In a simile the terms are explicitly related, in a metaphor one is often implied through the other. The relationship need not be analysed or consciously perceived by the reader in order for him to appreciate the image.

POETIC IMAGERY

It is not necessary to expand 'Your words will sting' to 'Your words will hurt his mind as a sting would his body', and the fact that a relationship is implied may not be noticed. The relationship between the terms is made not to direct attention to the analogy, or necessarily to suggest a mental image, but in order to intensify emotionally the basic idea, and through the associations of feeling and of sense to direct, by limiting or enlarging, its meaning; hence, perhaps, in some measure to recreate its meaning. Another aspect of the poetic image is its compression of language or of associations as a means of obtaining emotional intensification. Many more words than an image contains are usually required in order to paraphrase it. This is as true of the long epic simile as it is of the briefest metaphor, and the difference between the two seems to be one of emotional pitch: one is common in narrative, reflective or epic poetry, the other in shorter, more intense forms, in much lyric verse, in the drama, which is a succession of short passages given to different characters, and especially in tragedy, which is keyed at a very high emotional level. In order to be successful, the poetic image needs to have sufficient sensuous appeal or novelty to arrest the reader's attention and stir his imagination. A means to achieve this is by the presentation of a lively visual or kinaesthetic image; another means is by giving movement to something immobile or dead. This requirement is again connected with emotional intensification: by common use and frequent repetition some images lose this quality of intensification, and as 'dead metaphors' cease to be of use in poetry. Even these, however, may be brought to life again in a fresh context. The terms of an image need to be appropriate to each other to the extent that the basic idea, the tenor (object-matter), is emotionally realized; such appropriateness seems to be governed by the quality of the image in its context, and no limits can be stated. The point of contact between the terms must be emotionally fitting, but may be quite remote, and only terms which have no point of contact at all, if there are any, cannot be combined in a poetic image.

POETIC IMAGERY

If these points, most of which are commonplace, be allowed, it may be possible to frame a rough definition of a poetic image, metaphor and simile, in the following way: an image is a relationship, though not necessarily an analogy, explicit or implied, between two or more terms, made so that one term or set of terms (the tenor or object-matter) is given an emotional colouring, and its imaginative meaning, though not often its literal sense, is intensified, directed, perhaps to some extent recreated, through its association or identification with the other term or terms (the vehicle or subject-matter). Like the others, this definition is not exclusive; it is not a definition of metaphor and simile alone. It would include allegory, personification, symbolic description and narrative like that of *The Rime of the Ancient Mariner* or *The Love Song of J. Alfred Prufrock*, which seems to be a kind of sustained subject-matter; in these poems, the main term of the image, the tenor, the spiritual experience which the central figures undergo, is implied or suggested through the actions attributed to them. At the same time, this definition is more explicit and full than most of those given above, and perhaps serves to show that to define metaphor in other than mechanical terms is to approach towards a definition of poetry itself: for it would embrace many of those numerous figures of speech or of thought detailed, for instance, by the Elizabethan rhetoricians in their arts of poetry. Metaphor is merely one, the most concentrated and most striking, of many devices in poetry which do the same work.

When attention is directed towards the relationship between the terms rather than to the word-picture they may evoke or the analogy that may be found, it becomes clear that there are many kinds of poetic image. Concentration on metaphor in a narrow sense has led to a devaluation of poetry which does not employ it, as shown in the explanations offered for the difference between the intellectual imagery of a poet like Donne, and the more sensuous imagery of a poet like Shelley. It is often said or implied that the imagery of Donne is entirely functional, whereas sensuous imagery is merely decorative[1]; or an explanation is made in terms of quality, that the imagery of the metaphysical poets is good, while that of many other poets is bad; or again, a comparison is drawn between the complexity, maturity and intelligence of metaphysical poetry, and the failure to survive an ironical contemplation, the immaturity, the sentimentality of poetry which 'depends for its success on inducing a kind of attention that doesn't bring the critical intelligence into play'.[2] There seems little doubt that a real difference exists: in images such as

> *Put rancours in the vessel of my peace,*
> *(Macbeth*, III.i.67)
>
> *The thought of him rubs heaven in thy way,*
> *(The Revenger's Tragedy*, III.v.224)

the sensuous effect is unimportant, and the power of the metaphors lies in the novelty of the relationships established and the imaginative vigour with which these are made. On the other hand, the sensuous effect, the mental picture suggested, is very important in the following images:

> *But look, the morn in russet mantle clad*
> *Walks o'er the dew of yon high eastward hill.*
> *(Hamlet*, I.i.166)
>
> *It visits with inconstant glance*
> *Each human heart and countenance;*
> *Like hues and harmonies of evening,—*
> *Like clouds in starlight widely spread . . .*
> *(Hymn to Intellectual Beauty*, Stanza 1)

These deliberately seek to recreate in the reader feelings associated with the beauty of the natural scene, dawn, sunset,

---

[1] As by Alice S. Brandenburg, who contrasts the 'dynamic' imagery of the metaphysical poets with the 'static' imagery of the Elizabethan sonnetteers; see *PMLA*, LVII (1942), 1041.

[2] F. R. Leavis, *Revaluation* (1936), p. 207, referring to Shelley. For a review of the attacks on Shelley, and a general defence of the kind of poetry he writes, see F. A. Pottle, 'The Case of Shelley', *PMLA*, LXVII (1952), 589-608. and cf. C. S. Lewis, *Rehabilitations* (1939), pp. 1-34.

POETIC IMAGERY

starlight, the first passage in order to relieve tension after the appearance of the Ghost, the second looking for a remote yet familiar correlative for a difficult and abstract concept. Both kinds of image are functional in their contexts, but they are different in character: one kind may be called an image of thought, the other an image of impression.

The image of thought seems to work by bringing directly to life, making active, the relationship between the terms, which are usually fully stated, and contain the meaning of the image. These terms may be abstract words, as in

> *How all occasions do inform against me,*
> *And spur my dull revenge.*
> (*Hamlet*, IV.iv.32)
>
> *Virtue itself scapes not calumnious strokes.*
> (*Hamlet*, I.iii.38)

There is no word-picture, or what there is matters little; even those images of thought which seem to offer some kind of word-picture do so not in order that we may contemplate it and commit ourselves to its evocative power, but in order to startle us into a new awareness of the relationship involved. There is no natural or traditional connexion between such word-pictures and the tenor of the image, but rather an opposition, so that the effect is one of ingenuity or wit: two famous examples will serve:

> *If they be two, they are two so*
> *As stiff twin compasses be two;*
> *Thy soul, the fix'd foot, makes no show*
> *To move, but doth if th'other do.*
> (*A Valediction: Forbidding Mourning*)
>
> *Where the evening is spread out against the sky*
> *Like a patient etherized upon a table.*
> (*The Love-Song of J. Alfred Prufrock*)

The word-pictures in these images have no established

emotive value; their appeal lies in the novelty, the originality of the connexions they establish.

Originality in this sense of seeking a new way of expressing a relationship, or seeking a new relationship, one never made before, is characteristic of the brief image of thought: it works by direct interaction of human attributes, feelings, ideas or persons, and the figurative quality of such images lies in the novel way in which relationships are realized, usually in terms of concrete objects, or in terms of the attribution of action or life to abstract ideas. Life and motion are the soul of the image of thought, which is seen in its greatest refinement in the swift realization of relationships by means of an active verb: Shakespeare provides many examples:

> *All pity chok'd with custom of fell deeds*
> (*Julius Caesar*, III.i.269)

> *Tomorrow, and tomorrow, and tomorrow,*
> *Creeps in this petty pace from day to day*
> (*Macbeth*, V.v.19)

> *an act*
> *That blurs the grace and blush of modesty*
> (*Hamlet*, III.iv.40)

> *Whereto serves mercy*
> *But to confront the visage of offence?*
> (*Hamlet*, III.iii.46)

In these the reader is not asked to contemplate a picture, but to be alert to and recognize in a flash the relationship involved, to share in a rapid mental action. The image of thought is dramatic inasmuch as it is concerned directly with tensions of thought and feeling, and it is especially suitable for and characteristic of intellectual poetry, poetry of wit, argumentative and reflective verse, and that lyric verse which dramatizes conflicts between the poet and himself, his mistress, or God. It is particularly common in the poetry of the 'metaphysicals', and in modern poetry. Being forceful, direct and brief, the image of thought is also the best medium for expressing the tensions between one character and another, and within the single character, in poetic tragedy.

The image of impression works indirectly by suggestion or evocation, and its immediate appeal lies often in a word-picture which we are asked to contemplate. In order to appreciate such imagery, we need to commit ourselves fully to the evocative power of the word-picture, and hence images of impression employ natural or traditional connexions between vehicle (subject-matter) and tenor (object-matter). Again two well-known examples will illustrate this:

> *As a huge stone is sometimes seen to lie*
> *Couched on the bald top of an eminence;*
> *Wonder to all who do the same espy*
> *By what means it could thither come, and whence;*
> *So that it seems a thing endued with sense,*
> *Like a sea-beast crawled forth, that on a shelf*
> *Of rock or sand reposeth, there to sun itself;*
>
> *Such seemed this man . . .*
>   (Wordsworth, *Resolution and Independence*)
>
> *As when* Alcides *from* Oelia *Crown'd*
> *With conquest, felt th'envenom'd robe, and tore*
> *Through pain up by the roots* Thessalian *Pines,*
> *And* Lichas *from the top of* Oeta *threw*
> *Into th' Euboic Sea.*
>   (Milton, *Paradise Lost*, ii.542)

Both of these images create word-pictures which exist in their own right, and have an emotional value in themselves: the first employs aspects of the natural scene, and relies on our familiarity with and community of feeling about that kind of scene; the second relies on our knowledge of and community of feeling about the torments of the hero Hercules.

These images are nevertheless original, but in a different sense from images of thought; their originality lies in the particular complexity and richness of application with which they are used, one to express the interinanimation of the natural scene and the living man which Wordsworth wants us to feel, the other to reveal how mixed with the most terrible pain is the rejoicing of the fallen angels at the apparent recovery of Satan. The material of these images may be used again and again, that of the image of thought once only. They do not depend on life and motion for their effect, but tend to present a picture that is static as a whole, even though, like a painting of a battle, it may be built out of action. It is out of this whole, not the individual details, that the meaning of the image emerges; it offers indirect imaginative realization of relationships, and the reader needs to contemplate the picture, which, if the poet succeeds, will guide him towards such realization.

In the image of thought both terms are fully stated, but in these images of impression, one term, the vehicle, tends to become elaborated into a full-scale picture, while the other diminishes to the bald 'Such seemed this man . . .'. The greatest refinement of the image of impression is seen in the omission of this term, the tenor, altogether[1]; it may be implied in the vehicle, or known through traditional associations. This is common in much allegorical, narrative and descriptive verse; an episode or story, the whole poem itself, may be a kind of extended subject-matter or vehicle, in which the physical events and the landscape portrayed relate to the spiritual state of the hero, or to the state of mankind, or to some aspect of human existence and its problems, only the poet has omitted the connective 'Such seems the human state on earth . . .', or whatever it may be, and has left us to make it for ourselves. Not that the poet gives his reader a free hand in interpretation; on the contrary, the context of the narrative directs the reader's attention to those relationships the poet wants him to realize, for, however remote the events and strange the localities described in the poem, the activities involved in them are representative human activities, such as travelling, hunting, fighting, types of all human activity; and

[1] W. K. Wimsatt noted this in his discussion of 'The Structure of Romantic Nature Imagery', remarking how 'The metaphor in fact is scarcely noticed by the main statement of the poem'; see *The Verbal Icon*, p. 109.

the landscape has its sun and moon, its day and night, its winter and summer, those features which have always been associated with man's nature or his span of life.

Such poetry often has no metaphor in the usual sense, and is analogous to that considerable body of lyric verse which likewise omits the object-matter, the tenor, of its imagery, or may do so. By this is meant verse which employs for its imagery objects or events in the natural world, flowers, the sun, the sea, stars, and so forth; these may be used again and again in the same way without losing their freshness, for their appeal is permanent, being continually renewed as a fresh experience in every generation. They tend to gather richer associations with repeated use, and come to embody a complex of relationships which do not need to be stated in the poem. Our familiarity with this complex of relationships enables us at once to interpret Herrick's 'Gather ye Rose-buds while ye may . . .' as something more than advice to pick flowers, and to recognize as far more profound than a lament for a dying rose Blake's poem

> *O rose, thou are sick!*
> *The invisible worm*
> *That flies in the night,*
> *In the howling storm,*
>
> *Has found out thy bed*
> *Of crimson joy,*
> *And his dark secret love*
> *Does thy life destroy.*

The apparent simplicity of many poems which employ imagery from the natural world, and have no metaphor in the usual sense, is deceptive. For although this imagery does not present directly tensions of thought and feeling, as do images of thought, it is concerned indirectly with such tensions. In much natural imagery a tension is implicit between the various feelings and ideas which an object has come to symbolize: the rose is an example, emblem at once of the most perfect loveliness, the beauty of womanhood, and of the swift decay of that beauty, of our

> *love of things so vaine to cast away,*
> *Whose flowring pride, so fading and so fickle,*
> *Short Time shall soon cut down with his consuming sickle.*

Alternatively there may be a tension between the object and man's common experience of it; an example is the salt, estranging sea, which is unpredictable in its behaviour, beautiful in calm, terrible in storm, a means of escape and at the same time a place of isolation, a constant lure and a frequent menace, familiar to most people, and yet perpetually strange.

The image of impression can be as rich and complex in its effect as the image of thought, but its complexity does not lie on the surface. It is the natural mode of long poems, and of much lyric poetry, of all poetry which is committed to a love, a faith, a world-order; it is the mode of *The Faerie Queene*, *Paradise Lost* and *The Prelude*, and of the lyric of acceptance. The image of thought is the natural mode of poetry of conflict, poetry which is uncommitted, in a final sense, though it may be striving towards a resolution of difficulties, towards an acceptance of a faith, like Donne's religious verse, or T. S. Eliot's *The Waste Land*. It is also a natural mode of poetic tragedy, where, however, it is merely part of a large organization employing many means towards a final effect which may include a kind of committal; the image of thought very nearly is the organization of the poem of conflict, which is necessarily short. The essence of this kind of poetry is metaphor; the poetry of acceptance may have little or none. On the whole this latter kind of poetry has always been the popular poetry, written for a public sharing the same kind of aspiration, or view of the world, or expressing an aspiration which would later become common. It is the accident of our time that elevates poetry of conflict, private poetry, written often for a circle of friends, or a small audience of intellectuals, to a prime status; and which gives authority to a body of criticism devoted to this poetry, to the analysis of metaphor, and hostile to poetry of acceptance. The rest of this study is concerned with the use of language and imagery in some Romantic and Victorian poetry, the poetry which, in particular, has suffered attack or near-oblivion.

[3]

ORDER OUT OF CHAOS
The Task of the Romantic Poet

THE Romantic poets wrote for a world which had changed greatly since the sixteenth, even since the early eighteenth century. Poets of these earlier times had been able to assume as their frame of reference a concept of an ordered and stable universe, organized in a system of degree ranging from God through angels, men and beasts to inanimate objects, a system in which man was the link between the natural and divine worlds, and in which the hierarchal structure of society corresponded to the ordered arrangement of the universe. This order did not exist in actuality, though it provided a prop or succedaneum for Tudor despotism, and might be seen as an ideal which society should attempt to fulfil; and indeed, much of the greatest literature of these centuries seems to grow out of the tensions between the ideal concept and the failure of life to correspond to it. This is represented for instance in the conflict between the King's party and the party of Edmund in *King Lear*: although the gods prove in the end to be just and order is restored, meanwhile the play shows powerfully the strength of Edmund and the evil daughters, who reject with contempt the ideal order.

However, the concept of order provided a frame of reference for literature. Actions, ideas, relationships of characters, were inevitably posed against an ordering of the world, a religious ordering in as much as it led up to God, which established their value and distinguished clearly between right and wrong, good and bad. Any story tended to acquire symbolic or allegorical significance in the light of this concept, and could be used to embody profound ideas and feelings about man and the world, could become topical in the largest sense. It is significant that most literature prior to the middle of the eighteenth century tells a story, or at least says what it has to say in terms of a world, events and people outside the author himself.

The concept of order was apprehended, it was thought, by the reason, which was regarded as the principal human faculty, the one which distinguished man from beasts, and which he shared with angels. Man, fallen since Adam fell, struggled to attain self-knowledge, and thence knowledge of God. The faculties of the rational soul, the reason, or power of judging between good and evil, truth and falsity, and the understanding, the power of comprehending things intelligible but not material, ideas, including the idea of God, had to be employed constantly to keep the senses in check and control the will, depraved since Adam. Then, passing from the first life in the womb through the second life on earth, men might be translated to heaven:

> *In this third life, Reason will be so bright*
> *As that her spark will like the sunbeams shine,*
> *And shall of God enjoy the reall sight,*
> *Being still increast by influence divine.*[1]

In a healthy mind the reason controlled the operations of the senses, and it was thought that the imagination, that 'general source of all our evils and disorderly passions',[2] on receiving impressions from the senses, 'changeth and rechangeth, mingleth and vnmingleth', coins all sorts of new and monstrous images, and is as easily receptive of the devil's illusions as of heavenly visions. It was regarded as a faculty men share with beasts, whereas reason was the prerogative of human beings; but as the mind of man was quicker than that of beasts, so his imagination worked to greater effect

[1] Sir John Davies, *Nosce Teipsum*, in Gerald Bullett (Editor), *Silver Poets of the Sixteenth Century* (1947), p. 400.
[2] Ruth L. Anderson, *Elizabethan Psychology and Shakespeare's Plays* (1927), p. 134.

THE TASK OF THE ROMANTIC POET

so that in trueth, *fantasie* [i.e. imagination] is a very dangerous thing. For if it bee not guided and brideled by reason, it troubleth and mooueth all the sense and vnderstanding, as a tempest doeth the sea.[1]

By the end of the eighteenth century the disparity between the ideal order and the world in which men lived had become so great, the ideal so meaningless, as to destroy its usefulness even as a myth. The growth of the middle class, of industry and trade, the decline of the monarchy and the aristocracy as representatives of power, and the approach of democracy were capped, for the early Romantic poets at any rate, by the French Revolution, Godwin's notions of a perfect society as a blithe anarchy, and pantisocracy. The old concept of an external order in the universe had gone, and was replaced by various ideas, which, like Godwin's theory, postulated the possibility of the self-fulfilment of the individual man as an ideal—the natural corollary to democracy; so Coleridge, welcoming the revolution, cried

> *And lo! the Great, the Rich, the Mighty Men,*
> *The Kings and the Chief Captains of the World,*
> *With all that fixed on high like stars of Heaven*
> *Shot baleful influence, shall be cast to earth . . .*
> *Return pure Faith! return meek Piety!*
> *The kingdoms of the world are your's: each heart*
> *Self-governed, the vast family of Love*
> *Raised from the common earth by common toil*
> *Enjoy the equal produce.*
> (*Religious Musings*, 309-12, 339-43)

The Romantic poets wrote for a society which could no longer be measured against a concept of order and degree, or by the standards of a mode of government fixed in a religious dispensation, one which was beginning to postulate the notion of self-government, of the equality of men. The destruction

[1] Pierre de la Primaudaye, *The Second Part of the French Academie* (1594), p. 156.

of an external frame of reference led them to seek a principle of order within the individual, within themselves, to write of man and the world largely in terms of their own inner life, or their own self-sought, self-created relationship with God. The point of reference in their poetry is the individual rather than society, or society seen as a collection of individuals, and not as an ordered hierarchy, and many of their greatest poems are documents of their own lives, *The Prelude, Don Juan, In Memoriam*.

The principle of order they sought was established not in terms of the external world and an appeal to reason, but in terms of the inner world of the individual, and an appeal to imagination. New critical attitudes and criteria were formulated to interpret and defend the new poetry, and received their finest expression in Coleridge's *Biographia Literaria* (1817). His theory of the imagination as the supreme unifying and creative power in the poet, was one aspect of a transcendentalism much less emphasized by modern writers who base their critical outlook on his; the imagination for Coleridge was that faculty which idealizes and unifies, the faculty by which we may perceive the unity of the universe, and apprehend God. It is not through Reason and self-knowledge that we approach the divine, but through the highest form of self-consciousness, which 'is for *us* the source and principle of all *our* possible knowledge'. It is through the individual consciousness, represented at its highest in the creative act of the imagination which repeats the eternal act of creation of God, that we perceive God;

> self-consciousness is not a kind of *being*, but a kind of *knowing*, and that too the highest and farthest that exists for *us*.[1]

This highest form of knowledge is possible only to a few, and only those who

> can acquire the philosophic imagination, the sacred power of self-intuition,

[1] *Biographia Literaria*, Chapter XII, Thesis X.

THE TASK OF THE ROMANTIC POET

will know and feel the 'potential' working in them, will be endowed with 'the ascertaining vision, the intuitive knowledge'.[1] The best poetry will have the quality of intuitive perception of larger unities, and will represent the highest form of self-consciousness of the particular poet. It then becomes permissible to judge a poem critically as an expression of an individual mind, an inner experience, and to define critical values in terms of 'originality' or 'inspiration', concepts commonly used to acknowledge the presence of some mode of intuitive perception. So Coleridge said:

> What is poetry? is so nearly the same question with what is a poet? that the answer to one is involved in the solution of the other. For it is a distinction resulting from the poetic genius itself, which sustains and modifies the images, thoughts and emotions of the poet's own mind.[2]

The Romantic poet employed the power of 'self-intuition' to restore order to a world which had ceased to afford ready-made images of order, in the way it had done for Shakespeare and for Pope. For Shakespeare the natural world (the macrocosm) was an extension of man's world (the microcosm), and the objects, beings, attributes of both could be used as touchstones of order and value, according to their place in the hierarchy. Just as the colour of a man's hair might indicate his character (for instance, the flaxen hair of Andrew Aguecheek), or his exclusion from the accepted order of society through deformity or bastardy make him a natural rebel (Richard III, Falconbridge, Edmund), so the natural world might also provide correspondences for temperament (as Othello, a native of a hot, tropical area, is passionate and hot-blooded), or accompany with appropriate disturbances men's disorderly acts (as night strangles day and the sun fails to rise after the murder of Duncan). Pope praised the 'amiable simplicity of unadorned nature' in his discourse on gardens,[3] and emphasized that art consisted in

---
[1] *Biographia Literaria*, Chapter XII.　　[2] Ibid., Chapter XIV.
[3] *Pope's Works*, edited W. Elwin and W. J. Courthope (10 vols., 1886), x. 530-3. The quotation is on p. 532.

'the imitation and study of nature', but his practice, like that of other landscape gardeners of his age, was to impose an order on natural scenery, even if it was an order, as in the contrived 'wilderness', derived from nature's wildness and not from geometry. In his poetry the natural world appears enamelled and painted as in a formal design, in which man's creations take their place, 'Rich industry sits smiling on the plains', and the 'ascending villas' on Thames-side suggest model planning. Nature is 'methodized' in accordance with an aristocratic scale of order and value in society, which in turn is given the sanction of divine law. In different ways, for both Shakespeare and Pope, the natural world was seen as providing a ready-made set of parallels for or images of human actions and attributes, as established in an order which reflected the order of human society.

The concept of ideal order in human society, the world of man, which had provided Shakespeare and Pope with a frame of reference, had collapsed and could no longer supply images of harmony for the Romantic poets; indeed, as stress was laid on self-intuition, self-consciousness and the individual imagination, human society became an image of waste, futility and ultimate disorder—so in Romantic and Victorian poetry the city becomes an image of spiritual exhaustion, or even an image of hell. The natural world also lost its order and its old emblematic function of providing a set of correspondences to the world of man, and took on a new aspect, offering in its wildness, as untainted by man, a refuge from disorder, and in its grandeurs, types of the sublime, images of aspiration. Natural objects, which seemed pure and permanent, or permanently recurring, in relation to the corruption of society and the transitoriness of life, were translated into symbols of the Romantic search for order, or into images of a spiritual harmony. Whereas for Shakespeare and Pope the natural world had reflected the order and values of man's world, of human society, an order attributed, it is true, to a divine dispensation, it now came to be used to embody the aspiration of the Romantic poet, to reflect directly a transcendental or

THE TASK OF THE ROMANTIC POET

spiritual order established by the imagination. Natural objects came to act as what Coleridge called 'conductors' of truths:

> the imagination . . . that reconciling and mediatory power . . . incorporating the reason in images of the sense, and organizing (as it were) the flux of the senses by the permanence and self-circling energies of the reason, gives birth to a system of symbols, harmonious in themselves, and consubstantial with the truths, of which they are the conductors.[1]

Whereas Shakespeare and Pope could use an accepted frame of reference as a touchstone of values, the Romantic poet had to employ his imagination to create one, and he wrote his greatest poetry when he succeeded in giving birth to a 'system of symbols' conducting truths. These might not even be truths of the same kind as those which Shakespeare and Pope embody in poetry, for the natural order to which these refer was taken as a norm *from* which the world and society (man in his fallen state) deviate in error or rebellion; but the Romantic poet attempted to establish a harmony such as the individual isolated in an anarchic society might attain by the power of self-intuition, that is, a possible spiritual order in which the individual might find an ideal, find repose from the world, and *into* which he might deviate from the norm. Since there was no common frame of reference to which the Romantic poet's system of symbols could be related, the truths which they might conduct were not always apparent, as is instanced by the famous review of *The Rime of the Ancient Mariner* as 'the strangest story of a cock and a bull'.[2] This difficulty was overcome in two ways, firstly by the use of images of impression, and secondly by the use of a vocabulary of value-words attached to these images.

By employing images of impression from the natural world, the poet could rely on traditional and common associations to enforce a symbolic value, and could use, to cite two simple

---

[1] *The Statesman's Manual*, in *Political Tracts of Wordsworth, Coleridge and Shelley*, edited R. J. White (Cambridge, 1953), pp. 24-25.
[2] Cited in *Lyrical Ballads 1798*, edited T. Hutchinson (1898), p. xxii.

examples, the rose as a type of beauty, mountains as emblems of aspiration. Inevitably some images proved so appropriate to the Romantic endeavour to tame chaos, to assert an ideal order, that they recur in the work of many poets. The most universal image is perhaps that of light, a fit symbol of spiritual illumination, of the transcendental vision, of the work of the imagination, or of the ideal to which the poet aspires. It takes many forms, but the sun, moon and stars are especially prominent because of their associations with heaven, their nature as permanent sources of light. So for instance, the sun and the moon are controlling influences on the voyage of the ancient mariner, and throughout Coleridge's poetry the moon in particular seems, as a light that shines in darkness, to symbolise the work of the imagination. In *The Prelude*, as elsewhere in Wordsworth's poetry, the sun and moon play their part, especially the 'deep radiance' of the setting sun,

> that deep farewell light by which
> The setting sun proclaims the love he bears
> To mountain regions.
> (VIII.117-19)

Again, in the climax of this poem it is the moon that reigns 'in single glory' over the grand vision in the last book. Keats wrote a long poem on the theme of *Endymion*, a human being spiritualized, made immortal, through his love for the moon, which again represents perhaps the power of the imagination; and the central figure of *Hyperion* is the sun-god. As Keats had appealed to a star as an emblem of permanence,

> Bright star, would I were steadfast as thou art!

so in *Adonais* Shelley's vision transmutes the dead poet into a fixed star, made immortal. One of the dominant images in *In Memoriam* is again light, and the restoration of faith in Tennyson is symbolized in the union of the evening and morning stars, Hesper and Phosphor (Section cxxi), both Venus, and both representing that love which had seemed

THE TASK OF THE ROMANTIC POET

destroyed with the death of Hallam, but is finally reborn in the morning light of a new assertion. All the heavenly bodies were types of 'that unchanging realm, where Love reigns evermore', and the pervasive image of light could well be made the basis of an anthology of Romantic poetry.

Light is one of many natural phenomena which provided images for the Romantic poets; indeed, all the forms of nature served as types of a permanence contrasting with the mutability of human life. So Coleridge said,

> all that meets the bodily sense I deem
> Symbolical, one mighty alphabet
> For infant minds; and we in this low world
> Placed with our backs to bright Reality,
> That we may learn with young unwounded ken
> The substance from its shadow.
>
> (*The Destiny of Nations*, 18-23)

This 'bright Reality', of the light that is a symbol of love and the intuitive experience of harmony, and is associated with the beneficial forms of nature, with all that is fertile or helps towards fertility, has its opposite in images of darkness, chaos and barrenness, amongst which the most important is perhaps that of the city.[1] For the city-dweller became a type of the man isolated not only from his fellows, but from those forms of nature which might lead him to a transcendental sense of unity with the universe:

> A sordid solitary thing,
> Mid countless brethren with a lonely heart
> Through courts and cities the smooth savage roams
> Feeling himself, his own low self the whole;
> When he by sacred sympathy might make
> The whole one Self!
>
> (Coleridge, *Religious Musings*, 149-53)

The city is peopled by savages, and the noble shepherds of Wordsworth's poetry are corrupted by contact with societies

[1] It has been briefly examined in W. H. Auden, *The Enchafèd Flood* (1951).

of men and cities. The poet called London a 'wide waste' in *The Prelude*; for the order, the harmony, which the Romantic poets assert is not one of society, but a transcendental harmony which the individual can attain only through communion with fit symbols, with what is beautiful and permanent, finding 'religious meanings in the forms of Nature'.

Another means these poets employed to establish this transcendental order was a vocabulary of assertion, of value-words representing concepts or feelings universally regarded as valuable, such as beauty, truth, liberty; words representative of the highest kind of bond between human beings, such as love, sympathy, harmony; words endowed by religious associations with a special sanctity, such as grace, ministry; or again, words expressive of the greatest human endeavour and aspiration, such as power, might, awful, sublime. These words and others which in their common use were associated with what men most value, with the loftiest hopes and ambitions, the greatest achievements, were used by the poets in connexion with images of impression. This vocabulary provided a context of values for the images, which take on a special character in terms of the value-words, for aspects of the natural world are endowed with the noblest human and religious attributes by their means. The effect is, in Wordsworth's phrase, to make

> *The surface of the universal earth*
> *With triumph, and delight, and hope, and fear,*
> *Work like a sea.*
>
> (*Prelude*, I.499-501)

Hence the forms of nature, the images of impression, become agencies by which these attributes may be transferred back to the poet's, and hence the reader's, aspiration, to the search for order. The process is again hinted at in the same book of *The Prelude:*

> *Wisdom and Spirit of the Universe!*
> *Thou Soul that art the eternity of thought!*
> *That giv'st to forms and images a breath*

THE TASK OF THE ROMANTIC POET

And everlasting motion! not in vain,
By day or star-light thus from my first dawn
Of Childhood didst Thou intertwine for me
The passions that build up our human Soul,
Not with the mean and vulgar works of Man,
But with high objects, with enduring things,
With life and nature, purifying thus
The elements of feeling and of thought,
And sanctifying, by such discipline,
Both pain and fear, until we recognize
A grandeur in the beatings of the heart.

The forms and images of nature are intertwined with human passions so that by a reciprocal action they are endowed with human feelings and with values, and at the same time the poet's feelings and aspirations are purified and sanctified. The value-words and the images reinforce one another, so that the images are imbued with the poet's vision, and the words become representatives of the truths for which the images act as conductors.

This vocabulary helps to establish the images in a 'system of symbols', and the images fortify the value-words and give strength to them when, as frequently, they emerge in passages of affirmation. Images of impression such as those noted, of light, the sun and moon, or the city, the desert, are relatively static symbols, offering little possibility of development as a structural basis for a long substantial poem. While they sufficed for a lyric or a brief notation of a poet's assertion, the long poem demanded a framework to give coherence and force to the images, to give them relation as a system of symbols; and long poems were necessary for an adequate statement of the vision, the assertion, because only a long poem allowed a full deployment of images and value-words, a sufficient context for them to interact richly, and lend complete authority and scale to the poem's affirmation. So the larger Romantic poems are given a shape which is governed and informed by a structural image, an action or theme which provides a framework integrating image and value-word, creating a system of symbols, and becoming the vehicle of the poem's final statement. These structural images, like the other images of impression, and the value-words, are rooted in a traditional way of seeing the life of the individual, or in a common experience of life. The most important are the image of life as a journey in time, and the image of love between two individuals as a type of a higher union.

It is out of these elements, images of impression, including the larger structural images, and the vocabulary of assertion, that the Romantic vision is built. The language of Romantic poetry works in terms of these elements, the study of which is the best guide to the true nature and quality of its endeavour to make order out of chaos.

[4]

THE UNFINISHED JOURNEY

Wordsworth's *The Prelude*

ONE characteristic theme of the Romantic poets is a voyage of some kind, undertaken usually by one man alone, often the poet himself. The nature of this voyage is best illustrated in certain short poems; two examples, both famous, are *La Belle Dame sans Merci* and *The Rime of the Ancient Mariner*. Both of these stem from the ballad, a kind of poetry which employed traditional symbols and images of impression rather than metaphor, and which was often concerned with a journey, or the effects of an expedition (as instanced in *The Wife of Usher's Well* and 'O where hae ye been, Lord Randal my son?'), and which for these reasons appealed to the Romantic poets. *La Belle Dame* begins with the figure of a knight alone in a winter landscape.

> *The sedge has wither'd from the lake*
> *And no birds sing.*

The harvest is over, and the season of death has come: the knight is pale as the lily, fevered, and the rose of his cheek is fading; so the opening stanzas set a mood of melancholy, and suggest through symbolic description that the knight is about to die, and that his youth and beauty have passed away. Then the knight answers the question of the first line, 'what can ail thee?', by describing his meeting with a beautiful lady, a sort of Circe figure, a faery's child whom he feels compelled to follow and love. He takes her on his steed, but does not know where they travel all day long, for she holds him with her eye, her strange songs, her strange words of love, so that he 'nothing else saw all day long'. The journey ends at her 'elfin grot', where he falls asleep under her magic charm, and has a terrible vision of kings and warriors in a kind of dance of death, their starved lips gaping; and he learns that like them he is enslaved by her implacable strange beauty.

The last stanza repeats the first, but between the two the knight has travelled not merely in distance from the 'meads', the natural landscape, to her elfin grot, a place of magic, and so to the cold hillside, but also in time and experience. She has led him from life to death, from the meads with their flowers, 'I made a garland for her head', their suggestion of spring or summer, to a desert of withered sedge with its cold lifelessness as of winter. The lady seems to be evil in the witchcraft she exercises over men, not requiting their love, but there is also a sense in which the knight accepts evil by yielding to her, putting her on his steed, and the movement of the poem is also from fertility to barrenness, from the acceptance of evil to an ignominious death. The poem has a cumulative symbolism which gives an enormous strength to the last lines, revealing, by its richness of implication, the final state of the knight as the last stage of a typical process of life, an enslavement of a man to a false beauty, a false love, leading only to waste and destruction. All the elements of the poem are old and valid symbols of the progress of life, and though we may read it without perhaps consciously thinking of their implications, our own past experience of life and literature is bound to guide us towards realizing them. In particular, the basic images of the passage of the seasons from spring to winter as a parallel of the growth and decay of men, and of a journey, especially a journey into unknown areas, as a type of the uncertain faring of humanity and the human consciousness through life, are familiar and renewed in each new generation.[1]

---

[1] There are other ways of interpreting this poem (see, for instance, E. R. Wasserman, *The Finer Tone*, Baltimore, 1953, pp. 65ff); my concern is to emphasize the character of the journey image.

WORDSWORTH'S *THE PRELUDE*

The Rime of the Ancient Mariner is more complex, and its symbols and meaning have received much attention; it would be pointless to repeat the detailed analyses which have already been made,[1] but some indication of the general pattern is necessary. The story again is of a journey; the ancient mariner travels south in his ship, at first in sunshine, but after the equator is reached, the control of the boat is taken out of the hands of the crew by a storm wind, which seems to carry with it a sense of evil,

> *And now the Storm-blast came, and he*
> *Was tyrannous and strong.*

They are driven into the ice and fog of a lifeless region, until the albatross comes like 'a Christian soul' to lead them out north again. But the mariner kills the guiding bird, goodness, and at once they pass into a stagnant, copper sea, where the ship cannot move, and everything rots,

> *And every tongue, through utter drought*
> *Was withered at the root.*

As in *La Belle Dame*, withering, barrenness, is a mark of death; the ship of death approaches, and all the sailors die one by one except the ancient mariner, who, long and lank and skinny, takes on the nature of life-in-death. He is left alone on the rotting sea until he blesses the water-snakes, when the albatross which the crew had tied round his neck falls off, and at long last he is able to sleep, a sign of peace and expiation of sin. The blessing continues in the return of life, the fresh wind which puts the ship into motion again, the birds of all kinds which accompany it, the rain which ends the period of drought and barrenness. The mariner falls into a trance-like state while the ship flies northward, and after learning as in a dream of the penance he must do, wakes to

---

[1] See Maud Bodkin, *Archetypal Patterns in Poetry* (1934); Robert Penn Warren, *The Rime of the Ancient Mariner* (New York, 1946) and W. H. Auden, *The Enchafèd Flood* (1951).

find that he is almost home. The curse on him is finally expiated as the troop of blessed spirits, which had inhabited the corpses of the crew and brought the ship back, ascends, the ship sinks, and he is taken off by a hermit and restored to his own land again.

This is only the barest outline of the poem's theme, but it points to some of the sources of its power. The mariner travels down below the equator to the underside of the world, traditionally associated with hell and evil spirits; at this lowest point he commits his crime, killing the albatross, and the expiation which begins when he prays is fulfilled in his restoration to the normal world, his return home to Scotland. In this sense the poem may be seen as reflecting a passage of life through sin, despair and degradation to a kind of redemption at the end. The icy waste of the frozen sea is, by implication, a place of evil, and once the crime is committed, the mariner has to suffer the barren heat of a still and rotting sea. As in *La Belle Dame*, the barren waste symbolizes a spiritual state; the poem's theme might also be described as the responsibility of the individual for what he does, going through a kind of dark night of the soul in suffering for sins: unlike the rest of the crew, who are irresponsible, alternately praise and blame him, and have no character or possibility of action except as a crowd, the mariner is given the chance to suffer and repent. Again, the sea itself is a place of loneliness, like the wilderness in the Bible, a symbol of man's experience as an individual set apart from his fellows, and also of that voyaging into the unknown which our lack of knowledge of the future suggests life to be; the old image of the end of man's life as a coming home to port is represented in Coleridge's poem in the return of the mariner to his home. It is possible to work out a much more detailed symbolism, to note for instance how things of good, the heavenly spirits, the albatross and other birds, the rain, are connected with the sky from which they come, while the sea is more often associated with mysterious things, the icebergs, slimy creatures, the water-snakes; or to identify the moon as a presiding, on the whole beneficent power as opposed to the sun which is often hostile and prevents the ship from moving.[1] However inadequate this slight account of the symbolism in the poem is, we have to interpret it in some such way.

Both *La Belle Dame* and *The Rime of the Ancient Mariner* tell a complete story, a fiction of a traditional kind, presented in a familiar ballad form, which beguiles the reader; they offer no difficulties of approach, and may be enjoyed simply as tales. But much of their power lies in the symbolic quality of the materials they employ. The images of impression from the natural world, the seasons, sunshine and storm, flowers, the sea, the barren waste, birds, rain, the sky, have been enriched by associative meanings through centuries of use; this latent richness is deployed in the context of these poems, so that a seemingly straightforward description contains a wealth of symbolic values which impinge on us even if we do not consciously recognize them or work them out. The basic image in each poem is one that derives from man's common experience of life as an unforeseen adventure, an unplanned voyage to an uncertain destination. This is man's experience of life as an individual rather than as a member of society, and the image of the journey of life is very characteristic of Romantic poetry which finds its inspiration primarily in the self-consciousness as a 'kind of *knowing*, and that too the highest and farthest that exists for *us*'.[2] Both poems are concerned with the individual; the knight and the mariner are set apart from their fellow men, as solitaries, and we contemplate them singly in their uniqueness; both poems also have a clear shape, a structure governed by the completion of the journey, of the life-cycle of the knight, who is left ready for death, and of the mariner, for whom no action remains, only a continued penance for what is past.

Many of the finest Romantic poems are incomplete; some

[1] These symbols are used in a much richer way than this simplified account suggests, and often seem to have a shifting or double application; cf. pp. 36-7 above.

[2] S. T. Coleridge, *Biographia Literaria*, Chapter XII, Thesis x; see above, p. 42.

were left unfinished, like *Christabel, Hyperion, Don Juan, Kubla Khan*, and Wordsworth's 'Gothic church', *The Recluse*; others are incomplete in a different sense, in the sense that there is no necessary structure dictated by the shape of a story, or by the exigencies of a set form. The most obvious instances are those meditative poems, usually in blank verse, and of indeterminate length, which were a favourite medium of Wordsworth and Coleridge in particular; perhaps the two most notable examples are Shelley's *Prometheus Unbound* and Wordsworth's *Prelude*. Of the first kind, those left unfinished, several cease in the middle of a story, as *Hyperion* does; in this the story was merely a vehicle for the real theme, which is not the wars of the gods, but the victory of a greater beauty, love and goodness over a lesser beauty, a type of the process of the poetic imagination as creative of new and excelling beauty. The story breaks off at the point where Apollo assumes godhead, and there could only have been one continuation, the ascent of Apollo to claim his rights from Hyperion, and Hyperion's eventual submission to a beauty greater than his own: this ending is already implied in the poem,

> *Mark well!*
> *As Heaven and Earth are fairer, fairer far*
> *Than Chaos and blank Darkness, though once chiefs;*
> *And as we show beyond that Heaven and Earth*
> *In form and shape compact and beautiful,*
> *In will, in action free, companionship*
> *And thousand other signs of purer life;*
> *So on our heels a fresh perfection treads,*
> *A power more strong in beauty, born of us*
> *And fated to excel us, as we pass*
> *In glory that old Darkness: nor are we*
> *Thereby more conquer'd than by us the rule*
> *Of shapeless Chaos.*

This speech of Oceanus is a key to the poem, the real action of which is complete in the fragment we have. Keats said that he abandoned *Hyperion* because there were too many Miltonic inversions in it, but there was a deeper reason than this; he had said all he needed to say, the effort was over, and to finish the narrative in that Miltonic diction which he had learned as a discipline to his fancy would have been a dull and deadening task—hence his statement, 'Life to him [Milton] would be death to me.'[1] A different type of unfinished poem is represented by *Don Juan* which is autobiographical in the sense that the central figure reflects Byron's own outlook and development: for this reason the story has no end, is amorphous and stops in the middle like human life itself; it has no necessary shape, except perhaps the shape of an uncertain pilgrimage.

The second kind of incomplete poem, as represented by *Prometheus Unbound* and *The Prelude*, is one in which the poet seemed to set out not from a narrative so much as from a set form. *Prometheus Unbound* was conceived as a drama of three acts, and it was not until several months after these were composed, according to Mrs Shelley, that the poet felt the necessity of a fourth act, 'a sort of hymn of rejoicing in fulfilment of the prophecies with regard to Prometheus'. This necessity was imposed not by the story, which is complete by the end of Act III, but by the real theme, for which the story serves as vehicle, that

> to be
> *Good, great and joyous, beautiful and free;*
> *This is alone Life, Joy, Empire and Victory.*

In other words, the set form of the poem and its true theme were in some measure at odds, and Shelley found it necessary to break the bounds of the form and go beyond the obligation of the plot in order to obtain a full statement of his theme. In its first form, then, *Prometheus* was unfinished, although it had the shape of a play.

The incomplete state of so many of the finest Romantic poems is a key to their true purpose and structure, their

[1] *The Letters of Keats,* edited H. Buxton Forman (3rd Edition, 1947), p. 435.

concern with the self-consciousness of the individual, the processes of the creative imagination, or the vision of an ultimate loss of identity in a unifying faith or love. The Romantic poets nearly all attempted to write in structures such as poetic drama or epic, which were not very suitable to their real source of inspiration. To be successful the poetic drama and the epic need to establish a group of characters existing in their own right in a world with a frame of reference external to the author, and thus to carry through a plot in which the characters seem to act autonomously. Shakespeare and Milton had a common external frame of reference which they could use, but the Romantic poets each had to struggle to create an alternative system for themselves, and their poetry is often an expression of this struggle. They found a new language, but clung to old forms; yet their best poetry transcends the limitations of those forms which conflict with the essential purposes of the poet, and the completion of the ostensible structure ceases to matter: we value the fragment, *Hyperion,* or the poem which overruns its form, *Prometheus Unbound,* for their achievement in embodying the author's vision. In so far as they do this successfully they create a new structure of their own.

Sometimes the chosen form and the poet's purpose coincided: *La Belle Dame* and *The Rime of the Ancient Mariner* are perfect because the structure of these poems was dictated by the story, and the story offered an excellent symbolic equivalent of the author's vision. The structure of the ballad is very well suited to the relation of a journey, which is the basic image of both poems, and which, as indicated earlier, is a characteristic image of Romantic poetry. The figure of a journey is a natural image of impression in which to embody the development of the self-consciousness, the soul, the creative imagination, common themes of the Romantic poets: their interest in figures such as Cain, the wandering Jew, Don Juan, and other travellers, is a reflection of this. The poets sought to fit the image of a journey to many set forms, drama, narrative, epic, not always successfully; the most interesting and the greatest of the poems which attempt this kind of reconciliation is Wordsworth's *Prelude*.

The Prelude is an unfinished poem in the sense that *Prometheus Unbound* is incomplete. It has a superficial resemblance to an epic in twelve books, and owes something in diction, structure, and perhaps in the religious colouring of its theme, to Milton's *Paradise Lost*, so that it has become common to speak of its 'epic structure'.[1] But *The Prelude* spills over into thirteen books, fourteen in the final version, and lacks that architectonic quality of *Paradise Lost*, the steady drive through a series of balanced episodes towards a predetermined conclusion, which is made to seem inevitable by the organization of the theme. Wordsworth wrote it casually, in fits and starts, and intended it to be the 'ante-chapel' to a larger work, *The Recluse*, which was never finished. It meanders loosely along, confesses to intervals between spells of writing,

> *Five years are vanish'd since I first pour'd out*
> *Saluted by that animating breeze*
> *Which met me issuing from the City's Walls,*
> *A glad preamble to this Verse . . . ,*
> (VII.1-4)

confesses also to a change of plan in the middle,

> *as this work was taking in my thoughts*
> *Proportions that seem'd larger than had first*
> *Been meditated.*
> (V.633-5)

The addition of another book to *Paradise Lost* would ruin the poem's shape, but it would make little difference to *The Prelude* if Wordsworth had added another hundred or two

---

[1] Ernest de Selincourt in his introduction to *The Prelude* (text of 1805), p. xi. Wordsworth's debt to Milton is discussed by Abbie Findlay Potts, *Wordsworth's Prelude* (Ithaca, New York, 1953), pp. 305-37; she concludes 'we can scarcely deny to *The Prelude* its place among English epics'.

hundred lines, especially perhaps at those places where, as he occasionally admits.

> *My drift hath scarcely,*
> *I fear, been obvious.*
> (V.291-2)

Indeed, he seems to have had difficulty at times in restraining himself from that anecdotal extravagance which mars the tale of Vaudracour and Julia; so in Book VI the account of his travels by Lake Como is broken off abruptly:

> *But here I must break off, and quit at once,*
> *Though loth, the record of these wanderings,*
> *A theme which may seduce me else beyond*
> *All reasonable bounds.*[1]
> (VI.658-61)

The real principle of structure in the poem is a journey as an image of development; it is a voyage in time and in space, of indefinite duration, and as on other long journeys, there are breaks, for refreshment, as it were, in a story or a piece of descriptive writing, for meditation on a particular prospect or theme, and for looking back to see the shape of what has gone before. All these may be relevant to the main thread of development, and the journey is still there to be continued after a pause. In an ultimate sense, it is the voyage of life, and the end of it is death, or some kind of defeat of death; the life-in-death of the ancient mariner or Keats's knight, or the triumphant vision of Wordsworth absorbed into

> *The feeling of life endless, the great thought*
> *By which we live, Infinity and God.*
> (XIII.183-4)

---

[1] All the passages cited here are from the 1805 version of *The Prelude*; some of them were omitted or altered in the version of 1850, but the main argument still applies.

WORDSWORTH'S *THE PRELUDE*

The progress of the poem, as Wordsworth was well aware, is meandering, like life itself; he compares it to the course of a river:

> *As oftentimes a River, it might seem,*
> *Yielding in part to old remembrances,*
> *Part sway'd by fear to tread an onward road*
> *That leads direct to the devouring sea*
> *Turns, and will measure back his course, far back,*
> *Towards the very regions which he cross'd*
> *In his first outset; so have we long time*
> *Made motions retrograde, in like pursuit*
> *Detain'd. But now we start afresh; I feel*
> *An impulse to precipitate my Verse.*
> *Fair greetings to this shapeless eagerness,*
> *Whene'er it comes . . .*
>
> (IX.1-12)

Not the poem, but life itself leads to the 'devouring sea' of death, and this image of the river, with its application both to the structure of the poem and its main theme, indicates a conception of *The Prelude* which Wordsworth had from the beginning, as a progress towards the culmination of life:

> *A Traveller I am,*
> *And all my Tale is of myself; even so,*
> *So be it, if the pure in heart delight*
> *To follow me.*
>
> (III.196-8)

This is one of the main thematic elements of the poem from the first book, in which it seemed to the poet that 'The road lies plain before me' (I.668), to the last, in which he wrote, 'the termination of my course Is nearer now, much nearer' (XIII.372-3).

The image of the journey operates on several planes, the simplest being the many descriptions of journeys which actually formed part of the poet's life, as for instance the journey to Cambridge (Book III), the return on vacation (Book IV), the travels over the Alps and into Italy (Book VI), into France (Book IX) and the final excursion into Wales (Book XIII). These are not simply literal accounts of travels, but mark a progress in time, in the development of the poet's imagination, and so interact with and pass into metaphors and similes of journeys, that they also come to act as images of impression. So, for instance, in Book III, the description of the poet's arrival in Cambridge, and his roaming 'through the motley spectacle' (ll. 29ff) there, is set off against the account a little later of his escape from the city to walk alone in the fields (ll. 97ff); the experience of Cambridge taught him to know himself and his powers, and the literal journey passes into and fortifies a figurative journey:

>   *it is enough*
> *To notice that I was ascending now*
> *To such community with highest truth.*
>
> *A track pursuing not untrod before,*
> *From deep analogies by thought supplied,*
> *Or consciousnesses not to be subdued,*
> *To every natural form, rock, fruit or flower,*
> *Even the loose stones that cover the high-way,*
> *I gave a moral life* . . .
>   (III.118-26)

The track pursued by the poet seems to be at once the literal 'high-way' of his wanderings, and the course along which his mind developed on the ascent to truth. The same double implication is often apparent, as later in this book when he says 'now into a populous Plain We must descend' (ll. 195-6), for this is literally true, connecting with the opening description of his arriving on the 'flat plains of Huntingdon' as the coach approached Cambridge, but is also an image of his giving himself up to social pleasures, neglecting his studies, and rejecting those who worked hard,

> *Willingly did I part from these, and turn*
> *Out of their track, to travel with the shoal*
> *Of more unthinking Natures.*
>   (III.517-19)

WORDSWORTH'S *THE PRELUDE*

This interrelation of the overtly figurative and the apparently literal image of a journey operates throughout the poem, and culminates in the ascent of Snowdon described in the last book, which is at the same time an ascent to a spiritual conquest. Perhaps the most striking example of the fusion of the two comes in Book VI, where, as the poet *wrote* of crossing the Alps, he was seized by an imaginative vision:

> *And all the answers which the Man return'd . . .*
> *Ended in this; that we had crossed the Alps.*
>
> *Imagination! lifting up itself*
> *Before the eye and progress of my Song*
> *Like an unfather'd vapour; here that Power,*
> *In all the might of its endowments, came*
> *Athwart me; I was lost as in a cloud,*
> *Halted, without a struggle to break through.*
>   (VI.521-30)

It is easy to read this passage without noticing that the vision does not belong to the moment of crossing the mountains, but to the moment of writing, for the image of the journey is carried on in the words and phrases 'progress', 'came Athwart me', 'lost', 'Halted', 'break through', and the associations of mountains are continued in the images of the vapour and the cloud; in addition, the attainment of the highest point on his road out of Switzerland, the summit of the mountains, is appropriate to the vision inasmuch as mountains are associated with aspiration, and to reach a summit is an achievement of danger and difficulty, or at least of effort and strain. So here the literal becomes figurative, and the actual journey over the Alps becomes identified with the progress of the song and the achievement of the vision.

The journeys described in *The Prelude* thus contribute to that figurative journey which is the poem's main theme, and what the poet said about his travels in Switzerland and Italy applies in some measure to them all:

THE UNFINISHED JOURNEY

> *whate'er*
> *I saw, or heard, or felt, was but a stream*
> *That flow'd into a kindred stream, a gale*
> *That help'd me forwards, did administer*
> *To grandeur and to tenderness, to the one*
> *Directly, but to tender thoughts by means*
> *Less often instantaneous in effect;*
> *Conducted me to these along a path*
> *Which in the main was more circuitous.*
> (VI.672-80)

The travels described in the poem relate to the spiritual journey which shapes it, and gives to it the character of a pilgrimage[1]; so Wordsworth addresses Coleridge,

> *O Friend, for whom*
> *I travel in these dim uncertain ways*
> *Thou wilt assist me as a pilgrim gone*
> *In quest of highest truth.*
> (XI.390-3)

In this aspect, the journey of Wordsworth is similar in many ways to that of the ancient mariner: he travels from his home, the happy landscape of his boyhood, through a desert of the spirit, like the barren waste where the mariner is forced to linger, to a rediscovery of the power of nature working in himself, and of his powers as a poet, and he returns home, to nature, changed by his experience. The journey begins in the valleys and hills of the Lake District, where as a boy he was subjected to the influence of the natural scene, and the first books describe

> *The way I travell'd when I first began*
> *To love the woods and fields.*
> (II.4-5)

In the valleys of peace and mountains of aspiration he found

[1] Abbie Findlay Potts, *Wordsworth's Prelude*, Chapter IX, relates the poem to Bunyan's *Pilgrim's Progress* and other literary pilgrimages.

a sense of identification with a larger unity, and grew 'Foster'd alike by beauty and by fear' to feel himself 'an agent of the one great mind',

> *I saw one life, and felt that it was joy.*
> (II.430)

A kind of stagnation came when he left school, home and the natural world for Cambridge, the university and city, where he felt a desolation of soul, as if he were rotting on a dead sea,

> *Rotted as by a charm, my life became*
> *A floating island, an amphibious thing*
> *Unsound, of spongy texture, yet withal,*
> *Not wanting a fair face of water-weeds*
> *And pleasant flowers.*
> (III.339-43)

Yet this was only a 'first transit' from

> *the smooth delights,*
> *And wild outlandish walks of simple youth,*
> *To something that resembled an approach*
> *Towards mortal business; to a privileg'd world*
> *Within a world, a midway residence . . .*
> (III.550-4)

and except for the interlude of 'transcendent peace' on his first vacation in the Lake District, where, on a walk in the mountains overlooking the sea, the poet became a 'dedicated spirit', the next books trace the poet's growing experience. His yielding to the 'vague heartless chace Of trivial pleasures' taught him the value of his own bringing-up, of the combination of book-learning and nature's lore, in contrast to the childhood of Coleridge, spent in the city,

> *Debarr'd from Nature's living images,*
> *Compelled to be a life unto itself.*
> (VI.313-14)

THE UNFINISHED JOURNEY

Wordsworth's own experience of the city follows, in his description of life in London, where after leaving Cambridge, he lived 'Single in the wide waste', and

> *pitch'd my vagrant tent,*
> *A casual Reveller and at large, among*
> *The unfenc'd regions of society.*
> (VII.60-62)

The central books of *The Prelude* deal with the poet's passage through these desert regions, through

> *the years*
> *That bear us forward to distress and guilt,*
> *Pain and abasement.*
> (VII.403-5)

Although he was fortunate in starting his journey with his 'face towards the truth',

> *Happy in this, that I with nature walk'd,*
> *Not having a too early intercourse*
> *With the deformities of crowded life,*
> (VIII.462-4)

so that his experience of the labyrinth of London, where 'the imaginative Power' languished and slept, did not destroy his faith in man, yet those 'deformities' were to bring a devastating shock to him. Books IX and X take him to France, where Wordsworth's early rejoicing in the success of the Revolution was soon modified, first by the intervention of Britain,

> *No shock*
> *Given to my moral nature had I known*
> *Down to that very moment; neither lapse*
> *Nor turn of sentiment that might be nam'd*
> *A revolution, save at this one time,*
> *All else was progress on the self-same path*
> *On which with a diversity of pace*
> *I had been travelling; this a stride at once*
> *Into another region.*
> (X.234-42)

Then the atrocities of the Reign of Terror brought 'a sense Of treachery and desertion', culminating in his loss of 'all feeling of conviction', his faith in nature and in man. The last books describe the final stages of the journey, the return to England beginning a process of restoration in the peace of the world, where

> Nature's self, by human love
> Assisted, through the weary labyrinth
> Conducted me again to open day.
> (X.922-4)

This restoration is completed in the great vision on the top of Snowdon described in Book XIII, with a renewed assertion of faith in man and nature, and in immortality, made more profound and valuable because it has been tested and earned by the poet's own suffering.

Something of the basic shape of the poem is indicated in this outline of Wordsworth's journey of development, a shape deliberately contrived by a rearrangement of events to form a fictitious sequence: the ascent of Snowdon which the poet probably made in 1791,[1] before the visit to France recorded in Book IX, becomes the appropriate symbolic climax and termination of a progress of the imagination, the spirit. It is a progress in which the boy's simple and solitary love of nature and self-identification with the natural scene, 'I saw one life, and felt that it was joy', is modified by life in cities, by contact with human love, suffering and evil (a process described in Book VIII, a retrospective view of the poet's growth of attachment to 'the good and ill of human life'); this more sober faith, after finding an object of attachment in the French Revolution, collapses in the succeeding Reign

---

[1] Wordsworth may have visited Snowdon when he stayed with his friend Robert Jones in North Wales in 1791, as is argued by R. D. Havens in *The Mind of a Poet* (Baltimore, 1941), pp. 607-8, or in 1793; in either case, if, as Ernest de Selincourt believes, the lines in Book X.792ff, referring to the French as oppressors, relate to Wordsworth's state of mind in 1794 or 1795 (see his edition of *The Prelude* (1926), p. 585), then the poet is here distorting the actual chronology of events in the interests of the poem's structure; cf. the note on the opening lines of Book I, p. 70 below.

THE UNFINISHED JOURNEY

of Terror, so that the imaginative faculty itself seems to die; and the progress ends with the regeneration of the imagination in a grander vision of love and unity. It is a progress from a simple faith through suffering and despair to a more profound and satisfying vision of man's relation to the universe, a journey of death and regeneration like that of Coleridge's ancient mariner.

So far the character of the journey as one taking place in space and time, as a voyage of life, a pilgrimage of the spirit in quest of truth, and a development of the imagination, has been noted. It has also a character in terms of descent and ascent. It begins among the mountains, symbols of the poet's aspiration and faith,

> *if in this time*
> *Of dereliction and dismay, I yet*
> *Despair not of our nature; but retain*
> *A more than Roman confidence, a faith*
> *That fails not, in all sorrow my support,*
> *The blessing of my life, the gift is yours,*
> *Ye mountains! thine, O Nature!*
> (II.456-62)

But soon there is a descent to the plains of Cambridge, which sucks the poet in like a whirlpool, with 'an eddy's force', and his sufferings, his acquisition of experience, take place on the lower levels of the plains, the sea, the desert, and the city, which shares the quality of these. For the city is a waste where all are 'melted and reduced to one identity' in a kind of 'blank confusion', and at one point Wordsworth's entry into it is compared to a passage into 'some Vault of Earth', a subterranean cave (VIII.711ff). In this suffering he learns

> *That transmigration could be undergone,*
> *A fall of being suffer'd, and of hope*
> *By creature that appear'd to have received*
> *Entire conviction what a great ascent*
> *Had been accomplish'd, what high faculties*
> *It had been call'd to.*
> (X.600-5)

WORDSWORTH'S *THE PRELUDE*

After this descent 'Through times of honour, and through times of shame' (X.943) there comes an ascent finally to 'highest truth', which also culminates in the poet's vision on the top of Snowdon, as he is restored again to the mountains. These various aspects of the journey and modes of Wordsworth's progress are all finally caught up in a passage in the last book, where he says of the imagination,

> *This faculty hath been the moving soul*
> *Of our long labour: we have traced the stream*
> *From darkness, and the very place of birth*
> *In its blind cavern, whence is faintly heard*
> *The sound of waters; follow'd it to light*
> *And open day, accompanied its course*
> *Among the ways of Nature, afterwards*
> *Lost sight of it bewilder'd and engulph'd,*
> *Then given it greeting, as it rose once more*
> *With strength, reflecting in its solemn breast*
> *The works of man and face of human life,*
> *And lastly, from its progress have we drawn*
> *The feeling of life endless, the great thought*
> *By which we live, Infinity and God.*
>
> (XIII.171-84)

All the various aspects of Wordsworth's development on this journey, the basic image of *The Prelude*, are expressed in terms of images of impression, drawn chiefly from the natural world. In particular, mountains, winds or breezes, the sun, the moon and light generally (as in the passage just quoted), are associated with aspiration, with the achievement of the vision, with the work of the imagination. The valleys among the mountains seem to represent havens of peace; islands, places where a temporary pause is made for rest and refreshment of the soul, or places of complete stagnation; and rivers are types of the progress of the soul on its meandering path. The desert, the city and the sea are forms of the wilderness through which the human spirit has to pass, enduring suffering and loss, in gaining that experience which enriches the final assertion. All these relate to the journey, and the various images interact in the poem's total effect.

This interrelation may be illustrated by a more detailed examination of the use of one of these images. The image of the sea is interesting, and is directly established in a relationship to the image of the journey in a passage of recapitulation towards the end:

> This History, my Friend, hath chiefly told
> Of intellectual power, from stage to stage
> Advancing, hand in hand with love and joy,
> And of imagination teaching truth
> Until that natural graciousness of mind
> Gave way to over-pressure from the times
> And their disastrous issues. What avail'd,
> When Spells forbade the Voyager to land,
> The fragrance which did ever and anon
> Give notice of the Shore, from arbours breathed
> Of blessed sentiment and fearless love?
> What did such sweet remembrances avail,
> Perfidious then, as seem'd, what serv'd they then?
> My business was upon the barren sea,
> My errand was to sail to other coasts.
>
> (XI.42-56)

The poet's 'business' in the central books of the poem has been to sail a 'barren sea', a voyage through a wilderness of spiritual desolation, which has to be endured before the shore can be reached. The sea is a vast medium of the spiritual voyage the poet has made, and, like most of the main images, it enters in the opening lines, celebrating Wordsworth's escape from the 'prison' of the city to the country, and his new liberty[1]

> Enough that I am free; for months to come
> May dedicate myself to chosen tasks;
> May quit the tiresome sea and dwell on shore.
>
> (I.33-35)

[1] This passage (ll. 1-54) was composed in 1795 before the rest of the poem, but this does not affect the argument here, for it describes an experience typical of the poem, and the images are appropriate to the rest of it.

The rest of the poem recounts the journey over that sea.

In the first two books, which describe his childhood, spent in the safe valleys of the Lake District, the sea is chiefly an emblem of might and sometimes terror. Splitting ice makes a sound like the noise of wolves 'When they are howling round the Bothnic main' (I.570), and when the power of nature most disturbs the boy, it seems to make the earth's surface

> *With triumph, and delight, and hope, and fear,*
> *Work like a sea.* (I.500-1)

The repose of the inland valleys is unaffected by the sea wind, 'Though wind of roughest temper' (II. 116); and at the height of his joy in nature, when he feels one life in all things, the sea is included with a 'yea' which indicates his respect for it,

> *all that glides*
> *Beneath the wave, yea, in the wave itself*
> *And mighty depth of waters.* (II.426-8)

There are other, gentler, references to the sea in these books, but the dominant impression is perhaps that at this period of childhood the sea represents a strange, vast, and unexperienced power.

The first sense that he has launched out on the sea comes in Book III, the story of his leaving home for the first time to study at Cambridge, which sucked him in as with 'an eddy's force' (III.11). Here his life became a 'floating island', luxuriant but rotting; he had been attracted by the fame of the town and university, but found life trivial there, and he warns against its siren-like appeal:

> *If the Mariner,*
> *When at reluctant distance he hath pass'd*
> *Some fair enticing Island, did but know*
> *What fate might have been his, could he have brought*
> *His Bark to land upon the wished-for spot,*
> *Good cause full often would be his to bless*
> *The belt of churlish Surf that scared him thence.*
> (III.496-502)

THE UNFINISHED JOURNEY

From this book on, the sea appears as an image of an experience of life which the poet has to endure. In a long simile in Book IV he compares his progress in the poem to that of a traveller in a slow-moving boat on 'the surface of past time'. Book V begins with the account of a dream in which the sea, the waters of the deep, seem to pursue an Arab as he escapes across a wilderness carrying his precious burden of a stone, symbolizing geometric truth, and a shell, symbolizing poetry; the dreamer, who had expected that the Arab would be a guide to 'lead him through the desert', sees him at last

> *riding o'er the Desert sands*
> *With the fleet waters of the drowning world*
> *In chase of him, whereat I wak'd in terror,*
> *And saw the Sea before me . . .*
> (V.135-9)

The sea here represents that necessary involvement in the life of the world from which it is impossible to preserve inviolate truth and poetry; but Wordsworth felt tempted to try, felt that he might emulate the Arab,

> *Could share that Maniac's anxiousness, could go*
> *Upon like errand.*
> (V.160-1)

There is another long image in the next book which relates to this; in it he illustrates the attraction the 'independent world' of mathematics exerts over his mind by the tale of a mariner, who, cast by shipwreck on an uninhabited island, finds that he can console himself and 'almost Forget' his misery in the study of geometry. This passage (VI.160ff) also looks forward to the time when Wordsworth was, as it were, shipwrecked in the sea of life, and sought in mathematics his relief (X.890ff.)

Meanwhile the journey has to be continued, as in a ship on a fair sea (VI.435), through the Alps into Italy, during the period of his residence in London and then his stay in France, a time culminating in the desolation of the Terror after the French Revolution. Even this had its 'bright spots':

> *as the desert hath green spots, the sea*
> *Small islands in the midst of stormy waves,*
> *So that disastrous period did not want*
> *Such sprinklings of all human excellence,*
> *As were a joy to hear of.*
>   (X.441-5)

But eventually the depravity of the times led to the poet's yielding 'up moral questions in despair', to the decay of his imaginative power; recovery from this critical stage of his development came on his return to England, whence he could look back on the time when his 'business was upon the barren sea'. His business there had been to learn the importance of living

> *Not in Utopia, subterraneous Fields,*
> *Or some secreted Island, Heaven knows where,*
> *But in the very world which is the world*
> *Of all of us, the place in which, in the end,*
> *We find our happiness, or not at all.*
>   (X.724-8)

So Wordsworth's journey, now almost over, has been invested, through the sea imagery, with

> *something of the grandeur which invests*
> *The Mariner who sails the roaring sea*
> *Through storm and darkness.*
>   (XII.153-5)

Much of the grandeur and meaning of the final vision are created by the image Wordsworth employs: the triumph of the imagination is represented by his ascent of Snowdon, which is also an ascent of the soul to a spiritual height on the mountain, overlooking at last the terrible sea, the sea of experience through which he has voyaged. This is the true end of that journey through the depths which is the heart of the poem, and the mountain is an image of his own mind in contact with the infinite, the sea an image of what has been overcome:

> *on the shore*
> *I found myself of a huge sea of mist*
> *Which, meek and silent, rested at my feet:*
> *A hundred hills their dusky backs upheaved*
> *All over this still Ocean, and beyond*
> *Far, far beyond, the vapours shot themselves,*
> *In headlands, tongues, and promontory shapes,*
> *Into the Sea, the real Sea, that seem'd*
> *To dwindle, and give up its majesty,*
> *Usurp'd upon as far as sight could reach.*
> (XIII.42-51)

The peculiar strength of this climactic image resides in the double recession of the sea, conquered and tamed beneath the 'meek' sea of mist, removed in depth and distance far from the poet, who seems to stand infinitely high above it. On this great scene the moon shines, an emblem perhaps of that light which the poet has at last attained; and a little way off the shore a chasm in the mist brings to his ears the noise of the sea,

> *the roar of waters, torrents, streams*
> *Innumerable, roaring with one voice . . .*
> *. . . in that breach*
> *Through which the homeless voice of waters rose,*
> *That dark deep thoroughfare had Nature lodg'd*
> *The Soul, the Imagination of the whole.*
> (XIII.58-65)

For the poet has completed his journey over the sea, has reached home, gained the shore, with a sense of lofty security; the 'blue chasm' links the conquered sea, the mountain and the moon as symbols not only of the poet's journey of the spirit, but also again of his ascent to triumph.

    These images of impression in *The Prelude* fortify and give body to the statements of the vision, of the assertion of the poet, which are necessarily vague, and are recorded largely in a vocabulary of value-words, whose function is to act as counters, as equivalents for what cannot be described, and so to work on our feelings. But for these to be effective, our feelings have to be wrought into a state in which we are prepared to accept the assertion they make, and the images of impression have to lend solidity and force to them, or they become mere empty rhetoric. In *The Prelude*, image and assertion reinforce each other fully, so that the great visionary passages are convincing. There is a complete sympathy between the value-words and the imagery, as is well illustrated by a passage cited earlier, describing the vision which came to the poet as he was writing about crossing the Alps:

> *Imagination! lifting up itself*
> *Before the eye and progress of my Song*
> *Like an unfather'd vapour; here that Power,*
> *In all the might of its endowments, came*
> *Athwart me; I was lost as in a cloud,*
> *Halted, without a struggle to break through.*
> *And now recovering, to my Soul I say*
> *I recognize thy glory; in such strength*
> *Of usurpation, in such visitings*
> *Of awful promise, when the light of sense*
> *Goes out in flashes that have shewn to us*
> *The invisible world, doth Greatness make abode,*
> *There harbours whether we be young or old.*
> *Our destiny, our nature, and our home*
> *Is with infinitude, and only there;*
> *With hope it is, hope that can never die,*
> *Effort, and expectation, and desire,*
> *And something ever more about to be.*
> (VI.525-42)

As noted earlier,[1] the account of crossing the mountains is carried over into the imagery of this passage, so that an experience which defies direct description, except in such

---
[1] See p. 63.

vague terms as 'visitings of awful promise', is given a specific character and value: the physical effort of gaining the summit is transferred to the achievement of the vision. The other images in the passage, of light—the light of sense extinguished in 'flashes' of a greater illumination—of harbour and home, all carry pleasant and valuable associations. The last two continue the idea of a journey from the account of the mountain-crossing, and suggest a culmination generally desired, in a place of welcome rest and security. So the images support the assertion, and the value-words, like 'glory', 'strength', 'promise', 'Greatness', 'infinitude', 'expectation', 'desire', 'hope', are given a focus, and in turn guide us to an appreciation of Wordsworth's experience here as something noble, important and valuable.

The repetition of value-words in different contexts of image and description also increases their effectiveness and lends them an aura of meaning. One prominent word of this kind is *power*. The 'objects great and fair' that afford a symbolic framework for the poem are often referred to as *powers*, so that this word becomes a means by which the natural world and the imagination, the symbols and the assertion, are integrated. The creative impulse is commonly described as a power, often with a capital 'P', as indicating the imagination; the intellect on the other hand is

that false secondary power, by which,
In weakness, we create distinctions.
(II.221-2)

The elements of the natural world are also called powers, like that of the imagination. Wordsworth begins the poem with an account of the first manifestation of his creative sensibility in childhood, when 'a plastic power Abode within me' (II.381), and in adolescence, when he felt that he was a chosen son endowed with 'holy powers' (III.83). In the context of these and other uses of the word *power*, it becomes clear what he means when, for instance, he says

WORDSWORTH'S *THE PRELUDE*

> *Of Genius, Power,*
> *Creation and Divinity itself*
> *I have been speaking, for my theme has been*
> *What pass'd within me.*
> (III.171-4)

The power is that of the imagination and of the natural world, whose

> *lovely forms*
> *Had also left less space within my mind,.*
> *Which, wrought upon instinctively, had found*
> *A freshness in those objects of its love,*
> *A winning power, beyond all other power.*
> (III.366-70)

Further aids to the development of the supreme imaginative Power are general truths, called 'Under-Powers, Subordinate helpers of the living mind' (I.163), and books, which receive Wordsworth's highest praise as

> *Powers*
> *For ever to be hallowed; only less,*
> *For what we may become, and what we need,*
> *Than Nature's self, which is the breath of God.*
> (V.219-22)

Books, like the forms of nature, foster the imagination in men, and both should be studied in order to acquire 'Knowledge not purchas'd with the loss of power', the poetic power that attends on nature:

> *Visionary Power*
> *Attends upon the motions of the winds*
> *Embodied in the mystery of words.*
> (V.619-21)

The poet's experience on the sea of life in London and France caused his imaginative Power to languish at first, but also brought about an enlargement of his sympathies, so that although he lacked his

> *early converse with the works of God*
> *Among all regions; chiefly where appear*
> *Most obviously simplicity and power,*
>
> (VII.718-20)

he gained enormously in other respects. He learned to love the 'Human Kind', to think of man as having at least the opportunity of becoming 'a Power Or Genius, under Nature, under God, Presiding'. He learned to distinguish the true poetic power from the 'adulterate Power', the fancy; and he sought a full expansion of his poetic faculties:

> *I sought not then*
> *Knowledge; but crav'd for power, and power I found*
> *In all things.*
>
> (VIII.753-5)

So he found even in the wilderness of London objects which engaged his sensibility, while he remained conscious that the strength of his imagination was due to

> *subservience from the first*
> *To God and Nature's single sovereignty,*
> *Familiar presences of awful Power.*
>
> (IX.236-8)

The middle books describe the impairing of his imagination and the last books its restoration; only through this experience did he learn the value and quality of the power he possessed:

> *I had been taught to reverence a Power*
> *That is the very quality and shape*
> *And image of right reason, that matures*
> *Her processes by steadfast laws, gives birth*
> *To no impatient or fallacious hopes,*
> *No heat of passion or excessive zeal,*
> *No vain conceits, provokes to no quick turns*
> *Of self-applauding intellect, but lifts*
> *The Being into magnanimity.*
>
> (XII.24-32)

WORDSWORTH'S *THE PRELUDE*

He hoped that his poem might embody his relationship with nature, might reveal the hiding-places of his power, and recreate for the reader the workings of the creative imagination, 'might become A power like one of Nature's'. The great vision from Snowdon in Book XIII is a recognition of the brotherhood of the power of nature and the power of the imagination; as he looked from the mountain at the forms of the scene before him, he felt that

> *The Power which these*
> *Acknowledge when thus moved, which Nature thus*
> *Thrusts forth upon the senses, is the express*
> *Resemblance, in the fulness of its strength*
> *Made visible, a genuine Counterpart*
> *And Brother of the glorious faculty*
> *Which higher minds bear with them as their own.*
> (XIII.84–90)

So the poem ends, having 'tracked the main essential Power, Imagination, up her way sublime', with this fine affirmation. The *power* which the forms of nature exert on the senses is identified as the 'express resemblance' of the *power* of the imagination, and this word, defined and enriched in meaning through repeated association with imagery, has become a means of making the strong assertion of this passage acceptable, of identifying image and assertion. The value-words and the assertions of the poem rest on the images of impression, and it is these which endow the abstractions with life. The nearest way for Wordsworth to embody his theme was in terms of a voyage involving seas, rivers and islands, mountains, valleys and deserts, the sun, moon and the winds, and other natural phenomena, which act as counterparts of the imaginative faculty or symbols of its growth through experience; these interact with the value-words to establish the grandeur of Wordsworth's imaginative achievement.

[5]

THE VISION OF LOVE
Keats's *The Eve of St. Agnes* and Shelley's *Adonais*

I

IN *The Prelude* Wordsworth celebrates the development of the imagination, that power which enabled him to 'hold communion with the invisible world', and gave him a sense of fusion with the infinite, of triumph over the

> *universe of death,*
> *The falsest of all worlds.*

For him, as for Coleridge, the imagination was above all a unifying power, a means to attain a faith, to perceive an overriding order in the universe. Much of their poetry, like *The Prelude*, is concerned primarily with the means (the imagination) by which order is perceived, but a great deal of the major poetry of the Romantic poets is concerned rather with the nature and quality of the order perceived. This is a distinction worth making because it is reflected in the character of the poems; the first kind degenerates at worst into a mere nest of abstractions, the second into a tedious tale. In the first kind, of which *The Prelude* is perhaps the supreme example, the vocabulary of assertion is prominent, words like hope, power, truth, beauty, love, abstractions necessary because the poet's aspiration, the agency by which he attained to a vision, could be described only in such terms as

> *The awful shadow of some unseen Power*
> *Floats though unseen among us . . .*

KEATS'S *THE EVE OF ST. AGNES*

In these poems images of impression prepare the way for, fortify and make concrete those grand and simple concepts which represent the poet's sense of a beneficent unity in all things, and which identify the power of the imagination. In the second kind, the vocabulary of assertion may be less noticeable, and subservient to an action, a story of a symbolic kind, which embodies this sense of unity. The supreme examples in this kind are perhaps *The Rime of the Ancient Mariner* and *The Eve of St. Agnes*.

The most common and characteristic concept representing the poet's sense of unity was love, the principle of harmony between human beings. The stated moral of *The Rime of the Ancient Mariner*, 'He prayeth best who loveth best', points to the heart of this poem; the mariner's sin in killing the albatross is due to a failure of sympathy with his fellow-creatures, and this is what he has to acquire through suffering, before his regeneration can begin. It is a gesture of love toward the water-snakes which enables him to pray,

> *A spring of love gushed from my heart*
> *And I blessed them unaware . . .*
> *The self-same moment I could pray . . .*

Love was also the motive-force of Wordsworth's imaginative power, which was fostered

> *By love, for here*
> *Do we begin and end, all grandeur comes,*
> *All truth and beauty, from pervading love,*
> *That gone, we are as dust.*
> (*The Prelude*, XIII.149-52)

But love differs from the other concepts with which it was commonly allied in Romantic poetry, truth, beauty, liberty, hope, in representing a relationship between beings: love is action, and is easily represented in a story, without recourse to the abstract idea. The fusion of identities in love is a type of that larger unity which the Romantic poets sought, a unity which would bind together a world that had disintegrated into a collection of individuals without ties. So Shelley defined love as

> that powerful attraction towards all that we conceive, or fear, or hope beyond ourselves, when we find within our own thoughts the chasm of an insufficient void and seek to awaken in all things that are a community with what we experience within ourselves. ... This is love. This is the bond and the sanction which connects not only man with man but with everything which exists.[1]

The desire of these poets for an ultimate order often finds expression in a vision of love, in which the value-words may be unobtrusive and have the function of enriching the values already implied in the action. Some of their finest poems are of this kind, and it is a characteristic mode in which Keats and Shelley in particular write.

Endymion, the first large-scale work Keats attempted, took the form of a vision of love. Through his contact with the moon, Diana, Endymion learns to be ambitious for more than merely 'the world's praises':

> *Wherein lies happiness? In that which becks*
> *Our ready minds to fellowship divine,*
> *A fellowship with essence.*
> (i.777-9)

If we can, by a species of magic spell, feel our way into sympathy with the gods, 'that moment have we stept Into a sort of oneness'; but there are richer ways to annihilate the self in becoming 'interknit' with others, and the supreme way is that of love:

> *But there are*
> *Richer entanglements, enthralments far*
> *More self-destroying, leading, by degrees,*

---

[1] 'Essay on Love', in D. L. Clark (Editor), *Shelley's Prose* (Albuquerque, New Mexico, 1954), p. 170.

> *To the chief intensity: the crown of these*
> *Is made of love and friendship, and sits high*
> *Upon the forehead of humanity.*
> *All its more ponderous and bulky worth*
> *Is friendship, whence there ever issues forth*
> *A steady splendour; but at the tip-top,*
> *There hangs by unseen film, an orbed drop*
> *Of light, and that is love: its influence,*
> *Thrown in our eyes, genders a novel sense,*
> *At which we start and fret; till in the end,*
> *Melting into its radiance, we blend,*
> *Mingle, and so become a part of it,—*
> *Nor with aught else can our souls interknit*
> *So wingedly; when we combine therewith,*
> *Life's self is nourish'd by its proper pith,*
> *And we are nurtured like a pelican brood.*
> (i.797-815)

In the last part of this passage Keats rings the changes on the idea of becoming one with something greater than ourselves, first in a succession of verbs, 'melting', 'blend', 'mingle', 'become a part', 'interknit', 'combine', and finally in the image of the pelican feeding her young with her own blood. The attainment of this state is the attainment of immortality through the destruction of the self, and Endymion goes on to say to his sister Peona that if earthly love can do so much, what then is the power of love among the gods, of the love between him and the moon:

> *Now, if this earthly love has power to make*
> *Men's being mortal, immortal; to shake*
> *Ambition from their memories, and brim*
> *Their measure of content: what merest whim*
> *Seems all this poor endeavour after fame*
> *To one who keeps within his steadfast aim*
> *A love immortal, an immortal too.*
> (i.843-9)

Before Endymion can reach that perfect state of happiness

which reduces all earthly pleasures to nothing, he has to suffer a kind of death; he falls in love a second time with one whom he takes to be a human maiden, and feels in his passion for her that he has been 'Presumptuous against love . . . against the tie Of mortals each to each' in thinking of a goddess,

> *I have clung*
> *To nothing, lov'd a nothing, nothing seen*
> *Or felt but a great dream!*
> (iv.636-8)

But mysterious powers have forbidden the maiden to be Endymion's love, and he recognizes then that there is nothing left for him but death. He may not resume his life as shepherd-king when Peona invites him, for he has tasted of higher than earthly joys, which, he says,

> *I may not see*
> *If impiously an earthly realm I take.*
> (iv.853-4)

So he prepares to die, appropriately at nightfall, and at the end of summer,

> *Night will strew*
> *On the damp grass myriads of lingering leaves,*
> *And with them shall I die; nor much it grieves*
> *To die, when summer dies on the cold sward.*
> (iv.933-6)

Only when he has accepted the idea of death, has 'drown'd Beyond the reach of music' in thoughts too deep for words, and comes to bid a last farewell to her, does the maiden reveal herself as the moon, Cynthia his goddess; and so, rapt into immortality, they 'vanish'd far away'. Enduring an experience similar to death was necessary for Endymion in order that he should 'by some unlook'd for change Be spiritualiz'd'.

The progress of Endymion is similar to that of Wordsworth in *The Prelude* inasmuch as both endure a kind of death and rebirth; in Wordsworth's poem the journey of life culminates in a profound vision of the unity of all things and a 'feeling of life endless', and in *Endymion* the hero attains immortality by absorption into a unifying love. The two visions are similar in kind. *Endymion* is not a very successful poem, as Keats knew when he said that it showed 'every error denoting a feverish attempt, rather than a deed accomplished'; it is verbose, slipshod, and much too long for a theme which is not properly worked out, which indeed hardly exists except as a framework on which to hang poetic phrases. The pattern of the vision of love contained in this poem is, however, interesting in relation to the poet's masterpiece in this kind, *The Eve of St. Agnes*.

This poem grows out of a series of contrasts. In the first two stanzas Keats uses every word he can think of, chill, cold, frosted, freeze, frozen, icy, to create a sense of coldness out of doors and within doors, so that the beadsman praying in the chapel seems to share the coldness of the world outside. The old monk hears music as he leaves the chapel, which might be church music, and this is the link—for music is common to the church service and to festivity—whereby Keats transfers his thought and our attention to the hall of revelry where chambers glow with light and warmth to receive a thousand guests. At this point in Stanza iv the beadsman vanishes and is not mentioned again until the very end of the poem. Apart from a sense of coldness these opening stanzas establish three main effects: one is the sense of being in a church, a religious atmosphere, conveyed by a heavily charged vocabulary, 'rosary', 'pious incense', 'sweet orat'ries', 'penance', 'sinners'; another is the idea of old age and death—the beadsman is one who has passed beyond the joys of life and has only death to expect,

> *already had his deathbell rung;*
> *The joys of all his life were said and sung;*

the third is the idea of prayer, of doing penance, as the old man stays awake all night 'for sinners' sake to grieve'.

THE VISION OF LOVE

The scene changes from the lone man in a cold chapel to a vast crowd in splendid rooms, from stillness to the bustle of the revels as the group bursts in and 'many a sweeping train' passes by. Even here the religious colouring is carried over in the detail of the 'carved angels', roof-bosses in the hall, to focus on the single figure of the lady Madeline. Although she is taking part in the dance, she is isolated from the revellers in her thoughts; she broods on 'St. Agnes' saintly care', on the legend she has heard of how on this night virgins may receive 'visions of delight' if they go to bed fasting, complete the 'ceremonies due', and pray to heaven for all that they desire. So Madeline, regardless of the revelry, and thinking only of the night and St. Agnes' promise, is created as a parallel figure to the old beadsman; both are set apart from the crowd, and both are concerned with prayer in the night to come. The opening stanzas have the effect of giving the folk-legend a fully religious colouring, so that what Madeline proposes to do seems a purely religious ritual.

Now Porphyro is introduced, the lover who has travelled across the freezing moors 'with heart on fire' for Madeline; again his adoration has a religious colouring, in his longing to gaze and worship unseen, and his prayer to the saints to give him sight of her. He ventures into the revels, among the hot-blooded lords who are mortal enemies to his house and lineage; like Madeline he is a stranger to the revelry, isolated, a votary, with a different purpose in life from the 'barbarian hordes' to whom he is an enemy. In all the palace he has only one friend, the old 'beldame' Angela, whose name continues the religious overtones. She takes him to her room, 'chill and silent as the tomb', a room of old age, of death, and agrees to help him in his stratagem to see Madeline in the night, upon his assurance that he intends nothing 'impious'. All their conversation is in terms of worship, and there is something holy about 'Good Angela', whose name echoes the phrase 'good angels' of Stanzas xiv and xvi, and whose prayers for Porphyro 'each morn and evening Were never miss'd'.

KEATS'S *THE EVE OF ST. AGNES*

At this point the action really begins, and the imaginary world of the poem is so well established that the ensuing story seems right and inevitable. One aspect of this world has hardly been mentioned, its strange magical quality that gives it an existence in and out of time. Keats learned something of his art to create this from Spenser, whose *Faerie Queene* he had continually by him, and whose stanza he adopts in *The Eve of St. Agnes*. For his poem Spenser needed to create a world of his own, different from the real world but analogous to it, and as complete in its own way as the real world; so that on all levels it could serve as an allegory of life, could be compared to everyday events, and yet would be too remote to put him in danger of being accused of malice, personal satire, or attacks on living people. In addition, to bring his knights to life, he had to display them in a variety of situations and undergoing a series of adventures. The stanza form he invented answered his needs admirably, and enabled him to build up the atmosphere of his faery landscape, where anything may occur, any kind of being be encountered, where castles spring up for the convenience of travelling and hungry knights, out of an endless countryside of mountain, forest, river and lake.

The stanza forms a unit, and the final alexandrine brings it to a firm close; so each stanza can be used as a step forward in a long poem, and nine lines allow a point to be developed and amplified. It gives a sense of leisure, compared with, say, the pace of the heroic couplet or ballad measure, and a sense of spaciousness. Because it is slow-moving it is not a measure for a short poem; it allows a poet to linger, to expand, to describe minutely. It had other advantages for Spenser, particularly in its rhyme scheme: the fact that each stanza has only three rhymes knits it as a unit, the more so because in the rhyme scheme ABABBCBCC the rhymes are intertwined. No pair of rhymes stands by itself, and in the Spenserian stanza there is no necessary break; it begins ABAB, but the B rhyme continues; it ends CC, with a couplet, but the C rhyme has already appeared earlier. By virtue of its interlacing rhyme scheme it offers great variety of stops and changes of rhythm; in particular it can become two quatrains, ABAB/BCBC/, with a powerful last line linking the two; or an equally natural break can be made after line five, ABABB/CBCC, dividing it into two unmatched sections, rather like a sonnet; or the couplet at the end may be emphasized by a stop before it. At the same time it preserves a unity, moves with a leisurely speed, and gives a sweet echoing effect through the repetition of its rhymes. It is a form especially suitable for detailed description; it lends itself to invocation and evocation, to sensuous word-painting, by the opportunities it offers for playing on repeated sounds. By its use Spenser successfully evoked his strange world of *The Faerie Queene*, and the finest passages in this poem are often those of lavish description, where the stanzas one by one create an aspect of the scene and mood, and by the richness of their sound and imagery, entice the reader into an involvement with the world they build up. In establishing this world, Spenser feasts the senses:

> *So fashioned a Porch with rare device,*
> *Archt over head with an embracing vine,*
> *Whose bounches hanging downe, seemed to entice*
> *All passers by, to tast their lushious wine,*
> *And did themselves into their hands incline,*
> *As freely offering to be gathered:*
> *Some deepe empurpled as the* Hyacint,
> *Some as the Rubine, laughing sweetly red,*
> *Some like faire Emeraudes, not yet well ripened.*
> (II.xii.54)

It is a world rich and solid in its details, which, as here, are made palpable to us, and vague in its outline; the proliferation of detail makes it real, though the colours are brighter and the sounds more ravishing than nature's, and the absence of a solid background has the effect of distancing it from the natural world, removing it from the laws of time and space, and giving it a dreamlike quality.

KEATS'S *THE EVE OF ST. AGNES*

Keats showed his admiration for Spenser's power to create a world at once substantial and unearthly in his early stanzas in imitation of *The Faerie Queene*, which describe an island fairer than 'all that ever charm'd romantic eye'. It was natural for him to borrow the methods of this 'elfin-poet' in creating the charmed world of *The Eve of St. Agnes*. The terrible coldness of the moors and the chapel, the noise and glamour of the revels, all the immediate setting is built out of an accumulation of rich details, and yet belongs to no period of time or geographical location: and a sense of enchantment is lent to the story by frequent allusions throughout the poem to elves, fairies and magic. So Madeline is shown as imbued with religious ardour in her determination to prove the legendary promise of Saint Agnes, and also as 'Hoodwink'd with faery fancy'. Angela thinks Porphyro must 'hold water in a witch's sieve, And be liege-lord of all the Elves and Fays' to venture in amongst his enemies, and he dreams of winning Madeline that night while

legion'd faeries pac'd the coverlet,
And pale enchantment held her sleepy-eyed.

The events of the poem have both a religious colouring and an air of enchantment; the first is part of their reality for us[1]; the second part of their remoteness, a means to remove them from subjection to the laws of causality, time and space. By the time the action begins, Keats has established this rich atmosphere, and has built up a series of contrasts of mood and values. The central figures, Madeline and Porphyro, are isolated from the crowd of revellers, in their pursuit of something beyond sensual pleasure. She is associated, through their juxtaposition in the opening stanzas, with the old beadsman, who, like her, is isolated from the world,

[1] That is, to the extent that this religious colouring is used to create a distinction between what is good and what is evil in the poem, to guide our sympathies and our moral attitude to the events and characters. In so far as it is an evocation of a vague medievalism, it helps, like the air of enchantment, to establish the remoteness of the action.

praying alone and doing penance for others' sins, in preparation for his death. Porphyro is directly connected with Angela, who is also cut off from the revellers by her love for him, and like the beadsman expects to die, 'Whose passing-bell may ere the midnight toll'. Both of these old people are associated with coldness, as opposed to the heat of the lovers and the hot-blooded dancers; both are holy and good, as opposed to the wickedness of the barbarian horde who would murder Porphyro even on the holy night of Saint Agnes, 'men will murder upon holy days'. So the opening in a chapel, the 'placing' of the beadsman and old woman in relation to the other characters, and the contrasts between coldness and heat, youth and age, goodness and evil, all help to surround the lovers with the sanctions of religion, as though what they are about to do is holy.

It is in keeping with this that Angela treats the lovers' meeting as a bridal feast, 'thou must needs the lady wed', and provides dainties for them while Porphyro prepares himself by kneeling in prayer. Madeline's bedchamber is like a church, with its triple-arched gothic window, its stained glass showing 'twilight saints', and herself, also kneeling pale in prayer:

> *on her hair a glory, like a saint:*
> *She seem'd a splendid angel, newly drest,*
> *Save wings, for heaven: Porphyro grew faint:*
> *She knelt, so pure a thing, so free from mortal taint.*

Her room, 'hush'd and chaste', is like the chapel of the opening, lit only by the 'pallid moonshine', and there is again a contrast between it and the noise and stir of revelry in the hall below, which intrudes just once into its peace (Stanza xxix). There is also a contrast between the pallor of the moonlight, reflecting her purity and chastity, and the crimson of the stained glass, which throws on her its blood-colour:

> *Full on this casement shone the wintry moon,*
> *And threw warm gules on Madeline's fair breast.*

The warm flush of colour is an emblem of the love she is preparing for, a love in which she is a saint, set off from the guilty revellers.

Now when Porphyro stands where she lies sleeping 'Clasp'd like a missal',[1] and sets out a table loaded with rich fruits and sumptuous dishes, he is bringing life and love into the cold, chaste room; with his 'glowing hand' he fills 'the chilly room with perfume light'. Then he wakens her from her charmed dream, 'Impossible to melt as an iced stream', by singing an old song, 'La Belle Dame sans Mercy', of the cruelty of unrequited love; and as she wakes, he kneels again in an attitude of prayer, 'pale as smooth-sculptured stone', like the sculptured knights of the first stanzas. He seems to her 'pallid, chill and drear', but the chill that lies on both of them is removed as, at her demand for the 'looks immortal' of her dream again, they melt into each other:

> *Beyond a mortal man impassion'd far*
> *At these voluptuous accents, he arose,*
> *Ethereal, flush'd, and like a throbbing star*
> *Seen mid the sapphire heaven's deep repose;*
> *Into her dream he melted, as the rose*
> *Blendeth its odour with the violet,—*
> *Solution sweet: meantime the frost-wind blows*
> *Like Love's alarum pattering the sharp sleet*
> *Against the window-panes; St. Agnes' moon hath set.*

The moon, symbol of chastity, has set, and the storm comes

---

[1] The continuation of this line, 'where swart Paynims pray', raises other associations; besides emphasizing the purity of Madeline, this phrase reflects on the ambiguous character of Porphyro at this stage. His proposal to enter Madeline's bedroom had caused Angela to call him 'cruel', 'impious' and 'wicked', and her fears of a rape may be revived in the overtones of 'Paynims', and of the eastern luxuries he heaps 'with glowing hand' in the 'chilly room'— these perhaps hint at a pagan sensuality, as well as life and richness. But such suggestions are discontinued as Porphyro is transformed; when he kneels by Madeline's bed, he is pale like the sculptured figures in a chapel; and in the achievement of love he completes a spiritual journey, is 'saved',

> *here will I take my rest*
> *After so many hours of toil and quest,*
> *A famish'd pilgrim,—saved by miracle.*

on, a magical, 'elfin storm from faery-land', to conceal their escape. Only at the very end does Keats place the story in time, 'aye, ages long ago These lovers fled away', and then it is no specific time, but rather that unspecified period outside human time when fairy tales take place, 'once upon a time'.

Perhaps the finest touch in the poem comes in these last stanzas, in the blending of the religious and magical elements. The consummation of their love confers a kind of immortality on Madeline and Porphyro, redeems them from their cold, death-like state, and spiritualizes them. It is a marriage, as Porphyro twice calls her his bride, sanctified and blessed:

> *Ah, silver shrine, here will I take my rest*
> *After so many hours of toil and quest,*
> *A famish'd pilgrim,—sav'd by miracle.*

It is in keeping with this spiritualization that they glide from the castle unseen, but there is also a suggestion of magic in the way they vanish, 'like phantoms', the doors, it seems, opening of their own accord:

> *By one, and one, the bolts full easy slide:*
> *The chains lie silent on the footworn stones;*
> *The key turns, and the door upon its hinges groans.*

Meanwhile the evil baron and his guests are troubled with nightmares of 'witch and demon', a phrase which brings the two elements together. The enchantment which surrounds the lovers is linked in this way to the religious sanctions with which they are endowed.

The last lines of the poem record the deaths of the two old figures with whom the lovers are paired at the beginning, Angela and the beadsman, on the same night that Madeline and Porphyro meet. The completion of their love is also a fulfilment of the lives of the old people, who have been awaiting death; and their death, at a time of blessing, corresponds to the release from mortality of the lovers, who, as it were, die into life by proxy, and achieve a spiritual state. Like *Endymion*, this is a poem about stepping 'into a sort of oneness' through the annihilation of the self; the vision of love is a vision of unity. But *The Eve of St. Agnes* is a much greater work of art, in which every image, almost every phrase, contributes to the total effect. It is built up out of a series of balanced and opposed images of impression; on the one hand, coldness, established in terms of the natural scene, is linked with old age; with chastity, and pallor, both symbolized in the moon; and with silence and death, imaged in the sculptured monuments; also with holiness, as suggested by the icy chapel and the chill chapel-like bedroom of Madeline. On the other hand, warmth is associated first with the noise and movement of the dancers, with bright lights and rich colours, then with the ardour of the lovers, and the new life which they attain, as symbolized in the glowing colours which are opposed to the moonlight in the bedroom. The traditional associations of things, for instance the sense of holiness and goodness that attaches to prayer and the attitudes of prayer, to a church, and hence to a gothic stained glass window, continually and subtly enrich the poem, and establish the spiritual quality of the lovers and the evil worldliness of the revellers. By means of these associations the simple story of Madeline and Porphyro is transformed into a vision of extraordinary power.

The greatness of the poet's achievement lies in this transmutation of an immoral tale, to put it at its crudest level, about a man getting into a girl's bed and eventually running off with her. Keats needed to make the story real to the extent that we are interested in and feel for the lovers, that we can relate it to our life, and unreal to the extent that we do not falsely apply the moral standards of everyday life, that we can accept the world it creates. So he placed the story in its own enchanted setting of a chapel, a castle and the moors outside, and left it otherwise unlocated in space or time. He was enabled to do this by the dreamy incantation of the stanza with its echoing rhyme, and by the evocative power of the detailed description to which the stanza lends itself; out of this description there emerges a complex of associations based on the initial contrast between the chapel, as related to Madeline's bedroom, the sphere of the lovers, and the castle, the halls of barbarian feasting. In this way a context is provided for the action and our response to it is guided so that we see in the union of Madeline and Porphyro a symbol of a universal unity, a sacramental triumph of all that is good, as through their love they are made immortal.

II

The value-words in *The Eve of St. Agnes* are part of the action, which itself contains the poem's assertion. Like Apollo in *Hyperion*, Madeline and Porphyro have to 'die into life' in order to achieve the vision of love and transcend their mortality. This process is analogous to Wordsworth's passage through the wilderness in *The Prelude*, and finds a parallel also in Shelley's poetry. In many of his shorter poems Shelley represents life as an 'unquiet dream', and his vision of an ultimate order in beauty or love follows a release from the despair or even physical anguish of ordinary life. Sometimes a natural process or phenomenon embodies this vision, as the natural world is untainted by men's misery, and full of objects which do not pass away, mountains, rivers, the sky, or things which reproduce themselves in continual beauty, and nature is often for Shelley a symbol of permanence to oppose to the mutability of life. So the *Ode to the West Wind* ends on a note of triumph in the identification of the poet with the wind as destroyer of past evil and preserver of good for the future, a triumph all the more powerful as a release from pain,

> *I fall upon the thorns of life! I bleed!*

In his other great ode, the joy of the skylark's song, a type of the spiritual and permanent, of 'Things more true and deep

Than we mortals dream', is set against the sorrows of this life,

> *We look before and after,*
> *And pine for what is not:*
> *Our sincerest laughter*
> *With some pain is fraught.*

Sometimes Shelley's assertion takes the form of a vision of love, as in *Epipsychidion*, which in some ways resembles *Endymion* and *The Eve of St. Agnes*. It differs from these in that it has only the barest outline of a narrative, and gains its effect through a sequence of idealizing images transmuting earthly love into an infinite passion. A youth's vision of 'the harmony of truth', which seemed to transform 'this cold common hell, our life', is embodied in the apparition of a maid; but the 'veiled Divinity' vanishes, and he seeks throughout the world for some form resembling hers. At last he finds her when she descends upon him like the moon upon Endymion, and puts him to sleep, into a state in which he is 'nor alive nor dead'. Before he can be united with her he has to endure a spiritualizing agony when her image fades temporarily, a dying into life:

> *What storms then shook the ocean of my sleep,*
> *Blotting that Moon, whose pale and waning lips*
> *Then shrank as in the sickness of eclipse;*
> *And how my soul was as a lampless sea,*
> *And who was then its Tempest; and when She*
> *The Planet of that hour, was quenched, what frost*
> *Crept o'er those waters, till from coast to coast*
> *The moving billows of my being fell*
> *Into a death of ice, immovable.*
>
> (308-16)

But the ice splits, the vision materializes, and 'from her presence life was radiated'. So they are united, she his sister and bride, in a mystical, and virginal, union that transcends mortality:

THE VISION OF LOVE

> *The day is come, and thou wilt fly with me.*
> *To whatsoe'er of dull mortality*
> *Is mine remain a vestal sister still;*
> *To the intense, the deep, the imperishable,*
> *Not mine but me, henceforth be thou united*
> *Even as a bride, delighting and delighted.*
> (388-93)

Meanwhile, as long as they remain on this earth, they will live on a remote island, where the only human beings are a simple pastoral people maintaining the life of the golden age. There, where

> *fields and woods ever renew*
> *Their green and golden immortality,*
> (468-9)

they will intensify their union and prepare under the influence of the permanent forms of nature for their ultimate loss of identity beyond death; then, 'Confused in Passion's golden purity', they will share

> *One Heaven, one Hell, one immortality,*
> *And one annihilation.*   (586-7)

In this poem the attainment of that vision of love which is 'An image of some bright Eternity' involves a release from the pangs of life; *Epipsychidion* celebrates the power of love over death,

> *For it can burst his charnel, and make free*
> *The limbs in chains, the heart in agony,*
> *The soul in dust and chaos.*   (405-7)

The process by which the final triumphant visionary note is reached is similar to that in the odes, but the poetic mode is different: in *Epipsychidion* Shelley sought to objectify his vision in terms of an allegorical narrative—the result is unsatisfactory because the narrative is not strong enough to give the poem a clear structure; in the odes he speaks in his own person, and the vision is not in terms of love but of his identification with a natural force, the skylark, the west wind, which is used as a running symbol throughout the poem. These two modes are characteristic of the way Shelley's mind worked, through allegory, as in *The Sensitive Plant* and *The Masque of Anarchy*, and symbol. He was much more conscious of the nature of his vision than was Keats, and also more self-conscious, less able to project it outside himself; he was always aware of his need to create

> *Forms more real than living man,*
> *Nurslings of immortality,*

and he sought deliberately a symbolic or allegorical mode in order to body forth the forms of things unknown. Consequently the projected vision, as expressed in *Prometheus Unbound* for instance, and the personal vision as expressed in lyrics like the odes, were not easily kept separate. They are related to each other, and ultimately form part of the same vision, but Shelley was not often able to create a world substantial enough to carry the projected vision, which remains dream-like, 'pinnacled dim in the intense inane'.

The greatness of *Adonais* lies in its fusion of the projected and personal visions into one whole with a clear structure and dramatic flow. On one level the poem is personal, for Shelley did not care greatly for Keats as man or poet, but saw in his situation a parallel to his own. He created an image of Keats in his own likeness, 'a pardlike spirit, beautiful and swift', a genius 'not less delicate and fragile than it was beautiful'; this was how he liked to think of himself, as a beautiful, frail, lonely spirit on whom the reviewers and most of humanity poured abuse. The career and death of Keats, as he saw them, were analogous to his own career and probable death, and afforded a personal allegory through which he could explore again, as profoundly as in any of his other poems, the nature of his poetic intuition and of the vision of eternal love to which he aspired.

THE VISION OF LOVE

On another level *Adonais* projects Shelley's vision in the form of a myth, an impersonal mode, and in this also it is successful. Sometimes for his larger vision he combined scraps from his wide reading to make myths that he could use as vehicles for it; in this he was not often successful, for a mythical story needs to contain within itself its frame of reference. In this respect it differs from symbol and allegory, which may be explicitly identified with what they represent if the poet feels this is necessary; so the sensitive plant is identified, like the lady who tends it, in terms of 'love, and beauty, and delight' in the final stanzas of the poem named after it, and the skylark in the ode is compared directly to the poet. These have to be related to something outside themselves in order for them to be fully intelligible to us. But a myth as a story contained in its own world should hold within itself all the implications of its deeper meaning; that is to say, it needs to have found general acceptance, to have become part of the literary or folk consciousness of a people before it becomes of use to a poet like Shelley. When he creates his own patchwork myth as in *The Revolt of Islam*, the poem fails because the story refuses to shape the poet's vision into its unfamiliar terms. When he takes a well-known myth and treats it in his own way to shadow forth his faith that men can realize themselves to the full in love and liberty if only they will overcome the evil within them, the poem, *Prometheus Unbound*, is very successful. In his best poems of this kind he uses a familiar myth with an established meaning, and reshapes it to embody his vision.[1]

In *Adonais* Keats is transmuted into the beautiful young

---

[1] *Adonais* gains additional strength from its relationship to traditional pastoral elegy, and Shelley seems to have had in mind not only Bion's lament for Adonis and Moschus's lament for Bion, but also Virgil, Chapman and Milton's *Lycidas*. This is well brought out in an excellent chapter in E. B. Hungerford, *Shores of Darkness* (New York, 1941), pp. 216-39, and there is further discussion in J. A. K. Thomson, *Classical Influences on English Poetry* (1951), and in Carlos Baker, *Shelley's Major Poetry: The Fabric of a Vision* (Princeton, 1948). I have not dealt with this aspect of *Adonais*; my purpose is rather to stress the peculiar character of Shelley's vision in the poem, and the use he makes of the myth of Adonis, of imagery and value-words.

man of the seasonal myth who became the lover of Aphrodite-Ishtar-Venus, the great goddess of love and of reproduction in the world. In the myth he is killed, usually by a boar or a bear, and the mother-goddess goes into mourning (winter), until at her suit he is restored temporarily to life; then she mates with him again and fertility returns to earth (spring and summer). In the poem Adonais is beloved of Urania, his mother, who is at once goddess of love, for Urania was one name of Aphrodite or Venus, and the muse of astronomy,[1] so that she represents the idea of pure love and the idea of enthronement in the heavens. The mythical framework is established in the opening stanzas, which cry to all the world to mourn for the dead Adonais; and the end of the poem, his continued life in a bright and stable eternity, is already implied in its beginning. But the general appeal, 'O weep for Adonais', emerges out of the personal statement, 'I weep for Adonais', and the pattern of the myth corresponds to that characteristic pattern of Shelley's vision in the odes and elsewhere, of a 'dying into life', a passage through despair or anguish leading to a final assertion of faith.

The poem falls into three sections of roughly equal length.[2] The first, Stanzas I-XVII, calls on all things to mourn, and its burden is 'O weep for Adonais, he is dead'; Shelley uses all the resources of the Spenserian stanza to repeat and echo in different ways this note of lament. But the mourning is not unalloyed, for the verse already carries hints of the resurrection to come,

> *oh, dream not that the amorous Deep*
> *Will yet restore him to the vital air.*

At first the poem oscillates between these two attitudes, as

---

[1] Perhaps Shelley also had in mind Milton's address to Urania as the governor of his song, a superior muse of poetry, in Book VII of *Paradise Lost*; cf. Carlos Baker, *Shelley's Major Poetry*, pp. 241-2.

[2] It follows the usual plan of the christianized pastoral elegy, as represented in *Lycidas*, which moves from mourning for the death of a poet to a celebration of his renewed life in heaven. But Shelley's vision and his manipulation of the pattern are peculiarly his own.

THE VISION OF LOVE

in Stanza IV, where Shelley recalls Milton with the words

> *Most musical of mourners, weep again!*
> *Lament anew, Urania!—He died,*
> *Who was the sire of an immortal strain,*
> *Blind, old and lonely* . . .,

but the tone changes a few lines later with the assertion that 'his clear sprite Yet reigns o'er earth'. This counterbalancing of grief and triumph reaches its climax in the opposition between Stanzas VII and VIII, between the cry, 'Awake him not', because his rest is true peace, secure from the world's evil, and the lament, 'He will awake no more'. Then grief predominates for the rest of the first section, as Shelley uses the descriptive and evocative power of the stanza form to conjure up a pageant:

> *All he had loved and moulded into thought,*
> *From shape, and hue, and odour, and sweet sound*
> *Lamented Adonais.*

All Keats's visions and 'passion-winged Ministers of thought' pass in mourning like mist on 'an autumnal stream'; nature, the ocean, the winds, the seasons, and Echo having no more his songs to hear, all grieve. This pageant of the beautiful forms created by the poet and of the forms of nature brings to an end this section, which corresponds to the initial stage of the myth, the death and general mourning for the dead youth; and it is rounded off with a curse on those who caused his death.

The second part, Stanzas XVIII-XXXVII, seems to leap ahead in time,

> *Winter is come and gone,*
> *But grief returns with the revolving year.*

Like the first section, it oscillates for a few stanzas between grief, 'Woe is me!' and triumph, 'Nought we know dies'. Spring has come again and nature quickens into life, 'All baser things pant with life's sacred thirst', and propagate themselves under the influence of divine love; even the corpse of the dead poet is transformed into beauty and fragrance as it 'Exhales itself in flowers of gentle breath'; but the thought that all lives gives way to the thought that his spirit, his poetic inspiration, has vanished, and the cry to mourn now becomes fiercer than ever. Misery rouses Urania from her paradise to sing her lament, and his few sympathetic fellow-poets also come to bewail Adonais. As the first section ended with a pageant of general mourning, so this section ends with a pageant of the chief mourners, Urania, and the 'mountain-shepherds' Byron, Leigh Hunt, Moore and Shelley himself, and this too is rounded off with a curse on the murderer.

The second section thus parallels the first, and has the same structure, but it transports the action on to a new plane, and carries forward the idea of the myth. It passes from the general mourning of inanimate things, visions and dreams, to the particular mourning of Urania and the companions of Adonais; and it is only through their lament, through their understanding, that the transition to the final section of affirmation is made, and the assurance of life given. The third part opens with the cry that after all Adonais lives,

> *Peace, peace! he is not dead, he doth not sleep—*
> *He hath awakened from the dream of life.*

He has become part of eternal beauty, has become one with nature, one with Urania, herself the principle of love. Death is only a veil drawn across the light beyond, and now, instead of mourners, a pageant of immortals rises to welcome him as one of themselves,

> *the kings of thought*
> *Who waged contention with their time's decay,*
> *And of the past are all that cannot pass away.*

The poem culminates in the triumphant assertion that we

shall join him in an eternity of light, beauty and love if we can accept death as giving us shelter from the 'world's bitter wind'. The last three stanzas return to Shelley himself and form an invocation, a kind of prayer that he may be absorbed into the infinite, as he aspires to be where Adonais is.

The third section of *Adonais* is similar to the other two in structure, but celebrates the completion of the myth-cycle, the restoration of the dead poet to life, or rather makes the assertion that he enjoys a nobler existence beyond death. The three sections correspond to three stages of the myth, firstly, the death and general mourning; secondly, the lament of the special mourners, which is combined with a hint of a sacrifice on the part of the chief mourner,

> *Let me not vex with inharmonious sighs*
> *The silence of that heart's accepted sacrifice;*

finally, the granting of the appeal in the recognition that Adonais lives. As the first two sections begin with the cries 'Weep for Adonais' and 'Woe is me', so the last begins 'he is not dead'; the processions of mourners in the first two sections are related to the pageant of immortals in the third; and the curses with which the first two end are transformed into something like a blessing at the end of the third, Urania is not mentioned in the final part, in which the mythical element is slight. After the shape of the myth and of the poem is established in the first section, this theme becomes less and less prominent, while the personal element grows in importance, emerging unalloyed in the last stanzas. The change is marked in the different treatment of the figures in the second and third sections—in one the poets who mourn Adonais are presented in an allegorical disguise as shepherds, and are not named, and in the other they appear as in the life, Chatterton, Sidney, Lucan. In *Adonais* this emergence of Shelley speaking in his own voice is not, as for instance in *The Sensitive Plant*, a weakness of the poem, but part of its strength; for it grows organically as Shelley reshapes the myth to embody his vision, and the progress from death to renewed life is marked by the transition from the disembodied dreams of the first part, via the allegorical figures of the second, to the flesh and blood characters of the last. Explicit reference to the myth is not needed in the last section because the completion of the myth is implied in the first and because the last section grows structurally out of the first two and parallels them in its action.

Shelley uses not only a familiar story, but familiar imagery to shape and reinforce his vision of love. Most of this imagery is of the natural world. One aspect of it is seen in the connexions between the stages of the myth and the progress of the seasons, for in the poem death is associated with autumn and winter in the coldness associated with the dead Adonais, 'cold heart', 'cold head', 'frozen tears', 'icy lips', 'cold night', and in the comparison of mourners to autumnal mist,

> *the moving pomp might seem*
> *Like pageantry of mist on an autumnal stream.*

The first section ends with a fine image of the spring transforming herself to autumn in grief, but the second marks the transference of the action to a new plane with a movement forward in time to a real spring, 'Winter is come and gone'. Although this section fades into grief again as Urania rises 'like an autumnal Night', the resurgence of spring is an assurance of summer to follow, of the triumphant joy in every thing,

> *bursting in its beauty and its might*
> *From trees and beasts and men into the Heaven's light.*

The change of seasons is reflected more particularly in the recurrent image of flowers. The dead Adonais is seen as a flower faded before its time,

> *Thy extreme hope, the loveliest and the last,*
> *The bloom, whose petals nipped before they blew*
> *Died on the promise of the fruit, is waste;*
> *The broken lily lies—the storm is overpast.*

THE VISION OF LOVE

Urania sits in her paradise refusing to acknowledge his death, and listening to

> *the fading melodies,*
> *With which, like flowers that mock the corse beneath,*
> *He had adorned and hid the coming bulk of Death.*

This image of flowers sprouting out of a corpse returns at the beginning of the second section, but now without any suggestion that they 'mock' the dead, rather that the body renews itself in another kind of life. Now it is death itself that the flowers mock,

> *Like incarnations of the stars, when splendour*
> *Is changed to fragrance, they illumine death*
> *And mock the merry worm that wakes beneath;*
> *Nought we know dies.*

When the image returns again in the final section, it is as a symbol of the enduring beauty into which the dead poet has been absorbed, and Shelley urges us to go to his tomb in Rome, not to mourn, but to 'Seek shelter in the shadow of the tomb', to learn that death is rebirth,

> *Where, like an infant's smile, over the dead*
> *A light of laughing flowers along the grass is spread.*

The inevitable progress of the seasons reinforces the poem's structure, and is also an aspect of the permanence of the natural world. For, as commonly in Shelley's poetry, the uncertain and transitory quality of human life is contrasted with the enduring beauty of nature, which remains constant, as in the mountains and the sky, or continually renews itself, as in the plants. This is brought out at the beginning of the second section, where the death of Adonais is set against the renewal of the natural world in spring, and, for a moment, the poem drops into despair with the thought that all human beings must perish while the world in which we live endures and 'Nought we know dies':

SHELLEY'S *ADONAIS*

Whence are we, and why are we? of what scene
The actors or spectators? Great and mean
Meet massed in death, who lends what life must borrow.
As long as skies are blue, and fields are green,
Evening must usher night, night urge the morrow,
Month follow month with woe, and year wake year to sorrow.

Again, in the third section, the assertion that Adonais lives on is made in terms of his union with all that is permanent, with the spirit of love, which, though not given a name, is the equivalent of Urania, and

Sweeps through the dull dense world, compelling there
All new successions to the forms they wear;

and with the beauty that this love creates, symbolized in the eternal loveliness of nature: 'He is made one with nature.'

The permanence and beauty of nature are embodied in the central image of the poem, that of light, which also carries its traditional associations with knowledge, life and love. Light is connected too with Urania as the muse of astronomy, and the particular image of a star is especially prominent in the poem. At the beginning Adonais is seen as a star which soared into the sphere of human life and has descended into darkness; and that oscillation between hope for his continued life and grief for his death in the first section is represented in the contrast between images of ascent into light and images of descent into darkness. Poets, the creators of beauty, are luminaries in 'the night of time', the darkness in which most mortals live, an aspect of which is death:

Not all to that bright station dared to climb;
And happier they their happiness who knew,
Whose tapers yet burn through that night of time
In which suns perished; others more sublime,
Struck by the envious wrath of man or god,
Have sunk, extinct in their refulgent prime.

In this first part, the dead Adonais remains in the 'twilight chamber' of death, and the dreams and visions which come to mourn for him glimmer faintly in the gloom; so one is described in these words:

> *as a dying meteor stains a wreath*
> *Of moonlight vapour, which the cold night clips,*
> *It flushed through his pale limbs, and passed to its eclipse.*

In the next section the darkness is relieved as light begins to return. The flowers into which the corpse changes 'illumine death' like stars, and the visit of Urania to the death-chamber brings a little of 'Life's pale light' back to Adonais. But the note of grief becomes dominant again, and the image of the poet soaring and sinking like a meteor is repeated,

> *So is it in the world of living men:*
> *A godlike mind soars forth, in its delight*
> *Making earth bare and veiling heaven, and when*
> *It sinks, the swarms that dimmed or shared its light*
> *Leave to its kindred lamps the spirit's awful night.*

The expectation that light will return is fulfilled in the last part, in which Adonais becomes a fixed star that has 'outsoared the shadow of our night', secure in the heavens, a part of nature, of 'the loveliness Which once he made more lovely'. His light had only been eclipsed, not extinguished, and once the veil of death is torn aside, he is found enthroned in light, a type of the eternal beauty,

> *The One remains, the many change and pass;*
> *Heaven's light forever shines, Earth's shadows fly;*
> *Life, like a dome of many-coloured glass,*
> *Stains the white radiance of Eternity.*

Here the imagery of light emerges into an assertion of an enduring love and beauty beyond death, in the triumph of light over darkness, and the final stanzas, expressing

Shelley's own aspiration to immortality, end fittingly with another star image:

> *The soul of Adonais, like a star,*
> *Beacons from the abode where the eternal are.*

These images help to create and sustain the main theme as established by the mythical framework of the poem. Shelley used the Spenserian stanza not only, as Keats had done, for its descriptive and evocative power, but also with the allegorical machinery of *The Faerie Queene* in mind. Keats began from a simple theme of sexual love, which he made the vehicle for his vision by his power to set it in a world of enchantment and in a context of values which removed it from the plane of everyday life. He began with the fact ('Saint Agnes Eve—Ah, bitter chill it was!'), and had to transmute this into his vision: Shelley, as commonly, began with a transcendent vision, and his problem was to make it actual, to give it body. They went to Spenser for different purposes, Keats seeking a way of transcending the actual, of creating a faery world, Shelley looking for forms in which to embody the transcendental, and make his vision concrete. As in *Epipsychidion*, the love in *Adonais* has a curious virginal quality,

> *Like a pale flower by some sad maiden cherished,*
> *And fed with true-love tears, instead of dew;*

and though the relationships in both poems are nominally incestuous, they are relationships between apparitions, quite removed from the physical world. That between Urania and Adonais is made acceptable by its presentation in terms of Spenserian allegorical machinery, as in the pageants of shapes and 'mountain shepherds' who visit the dead hero where he lies in

> *that high Capital where kingly Death*
> *Keeps his pale court in beauty and decay,*

and also in the picture of Urania reclining in her bower and then speeding to the death chamber. The numerous personifications of Death, Corruption, Dreams, Echo, Ocean, the seasons, Memory, Desolation, Shame, and other abstractions, are also part of this machinery, which gives the right kind of life to Shelley's conception of the myth, a life abstracted from reality, but with a clear relation to reality.

This allegorical machinery moulds the story of Adonais to the shape of Shelley's vision; the death of Keats is treated in terms of the machinery as an artifice, and the reality to which it is related is Shelley's own state of mind and wish for a principle of permanence in life. Since the allegory in this poem consists so much of simple personification of aspects of nature and life, the transference from the allegorical world to the poet's own world is made particularly easy, and it never seems strange that Shelley speaks occasionally in his own person, a thing impossible for Keats in *The Eve of St. Agnes*. As the poem progresses, the personal note emerges more strongly to become dominant at the end; the death of Adonais-Keats belongs to the dream-world of allegory and myth, as do all the events of this life, and the personal note emerges with the assurance of love's fulfilment after death, so that, in the poem's terms, the imagined after-life seems more real than human existence.

The emergence of a triumphant sense of continued life at the end is marked by the development of a group of images not prominent earlier, images connected with fire and heat. As the death of Adonais is related to winter and coldness, to decaying fire or a 'dying meteor', so the final section brings a return of life and warmth; that spirit of love which is seen as the ultimate power, and into which the soul of Adonais has merged, the spirit

> *Which wields the world with never-wearied love,*
> *Sustains it from beneath, and kindles it above,*

is reflected not only in natural beauty and in light, but also in fire, a traditional image of love. The last section begins with the assertion

> *the pure spirit shall flow*
> *Back to the burning fountain whence it came,*
> *A portion of the Eternal, which must glow*
> *Through time and change, unquenchably the same;*

and the image of burning emphasizes the nature of the final vision as rooted in the unity of love. Images of light combine with images of fire, especially in the important star-images, as the 'effluence' of the good on earth lives on 'So long as fire outlives the parent spark', and the soul of Adonais burns like a star in heaven. These and the other main threads of imagery are gathered together in the fine penultimate stanza, which is the true conclusion of the principal theme of *Adonais*; it defines the nature of that eternity claimed in

> *The One remains, the many change and pass,*

and it expresses the poet's final acceptance, after the endurance of despair in this life,

> *Thy hopes are gone before: from all things here*
> *They have departed,*

of the process of dying into life. It is the grand assertion of his vision of love:

> *That Light whose smile kindles the Universe,*
> *That Beauty in which all things work and move,*
> *That Benediction which the eclipsing Curse*
> *Of birth can quench not, that sustaining Love*
> *Which through the web of being blindly wove*
> *By man and beast and earth and air and sea,*
> *Burns bright or dim, as each are mirrors of*
> *The fire for which all thirst; now beams on me,*
> *Consuming the last clouds of cold mortality.*

The assertion which emerges here strongly and simply in

terms of the value-words, beauty, benediction, love, is the climax of the poem. Whereas in *The Eve of St. Agnes* the characters are human, and the background unreal, so that the effect is of a real action in a mythical setting, in *Adonais* the figures are shadowy and the background, the death of Keats, the grave in Rome, Shelley's own relation to these things, real, so that the effect is of a mythical action set against reality. Thus the action of the former poem moves from the setting to the climax, which is the actual consummation of love in the union of Porphyro and Madeline, whereas the action of *Adonais* moves from the myth to the climax, which comes when Shelley is enabled to speak his faith in his own voice. One moves from setting to action, the other, as it were in reverse, moves from action to setting. In Keats's poem the physical union of the lovers is a representative human involvement in love, which becomes symbolic, in its setting, of dying into life, of transcending death, so that a statement of the assertion is not necessary. The action of *Adonais* moves towards the culmination of the myth, the achievement of immortality through love, which is made actual in terms of the last stanzas; the poem moves towards a statement of the assertion. For all their difference in this respect, the poems have much in common; in both the vision is projected into an action, in one an action embodying an assertion, in the other, an action supporting an assertion.

[6]

THE RHETORIC OF FAITH

Tennyson's *In Memoriam* and Browning's *Men and Women*

I

IN their finest work the great Romantic poets are concerned with asserting a principle of order and permanence in the universe. Whatever form their vision may take, it always involves some kind of absorption of the individual in a greater unity; it may be the apprehension of and sense of identity with the infinite in a moment of intuition, as in *The Prelude*, or the union of love, as in *The Eve of St. Agnes*, or the union with all that is good in a life after death, a dying into life, as in *Adonais*; it may also be the awakening in this life to the recognition that

> *He prayeth best who loveth best*
> *All things both great and small.*

The basis of this unifying vision is love, associated usually with beauty, truth, knowledge, liberty and goodness; and although the religious faith of these poets ranges from a Christian unitarianism to agnosticism, and varies from time to time, there is a common element in their poetic faith, namely the assertion that what is noble in humanity will endure, and the evil be purged away. In this lies much of the strength of their poetry; each poet in his own way faced what was for his time, and remains for ours, a central problem of life, the need for love and harmony in a society of individuals whose moral and social ties have decayed. The visionary power of their poetry is rooted in life, so that although it is a poetry of the individual self-consciousness, of the solitary set apart from society, it speaks for everyone.

This poetry of assertion inevitably employs rhetoric in order to persuade us that the poet's vision is real, and to make us believe in its power and value. It uses traditional and familiar imagery, particularly imagery of the natural world, which is often described in great detail, to evoke set responses, and bring us into a state in which we are ready to accept the visionary utterance when it comes. The familiar imagery informs this utterance and gives life to what is necessarily a vague and abstract appeal to a sense of unity in all things, an appeal often expressed directly in a vocabulary of abstract value-words. Wordsworth perhaps employs a wider range of value-words, and uses them more constantly, than the other Romantic poets, because so much of his poetry seeks directly to define and evaluate his own experience. But however indirect the recreation of the author's vision may be, as for instance in *The Eve of St. Agnes*, where it is projected wholly into a fictional narrative, at least the basic value-words, the roots from which all others stem, are likely to be found; that is to say, beauty love and truth. A remarkable use of this vocabulary is found in Shelley's *Hymn to Intellectual Beauty*, which inverts the Wordsworthian procedure of creating a context of natural imagery to support the abstractions which follow, and begins at once with the statement,

> *The awful shadow of some unseen Power*
> *Floats though unseen among us . . .*

The body of the poem gradually defines the nature of the power, of Shelley's intuitive vision, by means of a series of images which are involved with value-words. The main images are of light and shade, of natural beauty, and of harmony in colours and sounds. These have a double quality, first as types of a harmony that comes fleetingly to men, like clouds that pass on the wind, like the colours of evening that must fade, so passing into analogies for the transitory nature of life itself:

> *Ask why the sunlight not for ever*
> *Weaves rainbows o'er yon mountain-river,*
> *Why aught should fail and fade that once is shown,*
> *Why fear and dream and death and birth*
> *Cast on the daylight of this earth*
> *Such gloom—why man has such a scope*
> *For love and hate, despondency and hope.*

So light and harmony and beauty come to be associated with moments of relief from the darkness of human life, with love and hope as opposed to despondency and hate. Secondly the images, especially of light, which are central in the poem, represent a harmony that in another sense endures, since the light of day, sun, moon, stars, and all the phenomena of the natural world with which light is linked, continually return, or are permanently established. Hence the light and harmony which the vision brings are associated also with the conquest of 'Doubt, chance and mutability':

> *Thy light alone—like mist o'er mountains driven,*
> *Or music by the night-wind sent*
> *Through strings of some still instrument,*
> *Or moonlight on a midnight stream,*
> *Gives grace and truth to life's unquiet dream.*

The images confirm the value-words, love and hope, grace and truth, and help to suggest that life is a dream compared with the reality, the illumination of light in its traditional aspect as knowledge, which the vision provides. In this way the first three stanzas prepare the way for a change of attitude in the fourth, from assertion to prayer; they define the nature of the vision from the standpoint of the times when it is absent, 'Spirit of Beauty . . . where art thou gone?', but the fourth stanza transports us into the vision,

THE RHETORIC OF FAITH

Depart not as thy shadow came,
Depart not—lest the grave should be
Like life and fear, a dark reality.

While the vision remains, it alone is real, and endows the poet with immortality, but should it fade, death might become the reality. The prayer 'Depart not . . .' is answered in the last three stanzas, which sketch the poet's development; how in his boyhood, and in spring, the vision first burst on him bringing ecstasy; how he dedicated himself to the spirit of beauty, and all his joys and hopes have since rested in it. So by a kind of reciprocal process, the vision to which he has dedicated himself seems to become assuredly his in the final stanza, referring to his maturity;

there is a harmony
In autumn, and a lustre in its sky.

Harmony and light are permanent features of his autumn, his adult life; there is no more mention of the fleeting nature of the vision, visiting each of us 'with inconstant glance', and it is as if the poet, in accepting the spirit of beauty, and dedicating himself to it, has made it part of himself:

Thus let thy power, which like the truth
Of nature on my passive youth
Descended, to my onward life supply
Its calm—to one who worships thee,
And every form containing thee,
Whom, Spirit fair, thy spells did bind
To fear himself, and love all human kind.

Once again the images confirm the value-words; in itself the phrase 'the truth of nature' is meaningless, but the context of the poem has allied the beauty of nature, as represented particularly in light, with the poet's vision of permanence and unity; it is the forms of nature which contain the 'Spirit fair', and the truth of nature is the truth of the vision. This passage recalls the end of Stanza iii, 'Thy light alone . . . Gives grace and truth to life's unquiet dream'.

Throughout the poem the imagery supports the association of the vision with 'good' values, harmony, hope, grace, truth, love, beauty, and liberty, the

> *hope that thou wouldst free*
> *This world from its dark slavery,*

its bondage presumably to death, hate, as well as, literally perhaps, to oppression. The idea of liberty is introduced only in Stanza vi, and the process of defining the nature of the vision is completed only in the last line of the poem, in the notion of universal love, the compulsion upon the poet to 'love all human kind'. The unfamiliar and vague concept of the unseen power, intellectual beauty, is given substance and feeling by familiar images of the natural world and common value-words. There are other factors which contribute to this defining process, as for instance the religious terminology associated with the vision, words like 'consecrate', 'sublimer', 'dedicate', 'worships', which lend it an aura of sanctity; but the main achievement of the *Hymn* is the realization of Shelley's transcendent vision by these two means, the image and the value-word. They give life to the vision, and there is a sense in which the vision, in turn, endows them with life. For it is only the grandeur of the vision, its universality, embracing all humanity, and the poet's entire devotion to it, that as it were 'justify' the natural description and vocabulary of assertion, and enrich these with a range of feeling, an ardour they do not have in common use.

II

In such poetry the vision becomes reality, and the real world a shadow,—at best, as in the permanent forms of nature, it becomes a testament to the sublime life promised for humanity in the vision, at worst, as in the oppression and suffering of human existence, a transitory, dream-like state which has to be transcended. In the next generation of poets, Tennyson and Browning, influenced respectively by Keats and Shelley, create in their best work, *In Memoriam*, *Men and Women*, a vision of love, but of a different kind. For them, this world remains the reality, and the vision, detached from it, tends to become christianized into the new life of heaven after death, or absorbed into this life, as the fulfilment of a very real sexual love. The measure of the change is perhaps indicated by a comparison between Wordsworth's recovery of faith in *The Prelude*, which is assured in a moment of ecstatic vision on the top of Snowdon, in a sense of the one life within us and abroad, and Tennyson's recovery in *In Memoriam*, which is assured in a moment of communion with the dead on the lawn outside a house. For one the setting, the natural scene of the mountain of aspiration with the sea of conquered experience below it, was an essential part of the vision; for the other, the quiet lawn and fields where 'The white kine glimmer'd' were not much more than an adjunct.[1]

This change was inevitable, for Tennyson grew up into a world very different from that of the Romantic poets. It is true that he was enormously influenced by the 'new' contemporary poets of his boyhood and youth, Shelley and especially Keats—he began to publish (*Poems. by Two Brothers*, 1826) only nine years after Keats's first volume, *Poems* (1817), had appeared. He found in the poetry of Keats, as the Pre-Raphaelites were to do later, the representation of an ideal world, timeless and unchanging, a world of high romance or of art, set off from the real world; it seemed to be poetry of pure sensation, and it was this that he sought to emulate in his own *Poems, Chiefly Lyrical* (1830), if the review of his close friend Hallam gives any indication of the poet's thought. Hallam argued that poetry of sensation, as exemplified in the work of Keats and Shelley, was superior to poetry of thought, as exemplified in Wordsworth's verse;

---

[1] This is deliberate overemphasis, for purposes of comparison; see below pp. 132-4.

he went on to claim that Tennyson was a poet of sensation, and praised especially his luxuriant imagination, his 'picturesque delineation of objects' and the variety of his lyric metres.[1] The poems in this volume are nearly all concerned with remote or unidentified places and times; many words are used for their sound, rhythmic effect and power of evocation, rather than for their sense, especially the archaic or 'poetic' vocabulary which is very prominent, as for instance archaic words like wot, blosmy, zone (= girdle), or words evocative of the past, shallop, pleasance, aweary, coronach, and past participles accented on the last syllable, carven, flowerèd, or again, words which Tennyson almost made his own, like marish and sheeny. Most of the poems simply create an atmosphere or mood by their rich sounds, minute descriptive detail, and strange vocabulary, transporting us into landscapes bleak and bare, as in *The Dying Swan*, lush and overripe, as in the autumnal *Song*, or into a variety of moods, ranging from the wan listlessness of *Mariana* to the luxurious emptiness of *Recollections of the Arabian Nights*. They avoid reminders of the harsh world around us, and evoke a world of unchanging and purely decorative beauty, remote from life. Many of these poems have, within their limitations, an extraordinary power, which is largely due to their great technical virtuosity. The *Poems* (1833) continue the exploration of metre, rhetoric and atmosphere begun in *Poems, Chiefly Lyrical*, and again the best of them evoke a world of unchanging beauty, most finely in the setting of *The Lotos-Eaters*, 'A land where all things always seemed the same'. It is in such a world, created by art, that the poet seems to have found security from the 'damned vacillating state' of doubt in God depicted in *Supposed Confessions of a Second-rate Sensitive Mind*. This world is perfect in itself, as these poems represent magnificently one aspect of human experience, but it is sustained by no informing vision as were the worlds created by Keats and Shelley, and is an escape from, not a

[1] Cited in Edgar Finley Shannon, Junior, *Tennyson and the Reviewers* (Cambridge, Mass., 1952), p. 7.

solution for the problems of life. *The Palace of Art* shows Tennyson's awareness of this: his soul rejoices for a time in 'god-like isolation' from the world, but comes to realize that in her wonderful palace she

> Lay there exiled from eternal God,
> Lost to her place and name.

So the palace of art on its mountain height is renounced for a 'cottage in the vale', but, as the imagery of descent indicates, as well as the splendid description of the palace itself, it is a hard-won renunciation, and poetically seems a little forced; the last lines hint that it may in any case be only temporary. The quality of the verse suggests that Tennyson was really excited by the idea of the palace of art, a place of joy and song set apart from men, 'the darkening droves of swine' on the plain below. The romantic vision, in which the mountain is a symbol of aspiration to a unifying love embracing mankind and the universe, had begun to disintegrate.

There is little doubt that Tennyson was seeking in some kind of unifying vision a solution of the conflict represented in this poem between his desire for the security of a world of art, which proved ultimately to be a 'spot of dull stagnation', and his need for a faith which would involve the real world. Aspects of this conflict inspired some of the best of the *Poems* of 1842, most directly in *The Two Voices*, a dramatization of the debate in the poet's mind; one voice seeks to convince him of the wretchedness of this world, and the lack of intellectual grounds for faith in God, the other persuading that there is hope in the next world. There is no resolution, for although the poet is allowed momentarily

> To feel, although no tongue can prove
> That every cloud that spreads above
> And veileth love, itself is love;

yet gloomier thoughts return at the end. In *Locksley Hall* the speaker's vision of civilization progressing 'for ever down the ringing grooves of change' to a culmination in 'the Parliament of man, the Federation of the world', is contrasted with his own bitter experience as an individual,

> *Knowledge comes, but wisdom lingers, and I linger on the shore,*
> *And the individual withers, and the world is more and more.*

Material progress does not seem to be matched by a spiritual progress. The conflict is reflected also in the portraits of a saint afflicted with an ultimate doubt in *St. Simeon Stylites*, and the sinner given an ultimate hope in *The Vision of Sin*; and it appears in the battle between *Love and Duty*, in which 'Duty loved of Love' conquers, and love goes unconsummated in the not very convincing hope,

> *Wait, and Love himself will bring*
> *The drooping flower of knowledge changed to fruit*
> *Of wisdom. Wait: my faith is large in Time,*
> *And that which shapes it to some perfect end.*

These poems and others are concerned with the problems first raised in *Supposed Confessions*, the conflict between the visible signs of progress of knowledge, of science and wealth, and the failure of knowledge to bring faith or wisdom; between the poet's longing for security and failure to find it; between his desire for progress and fear of disorder; between his wish that all humanity may be saved, and his lack of faith that they can be saved; between his desire to believe in the overruling efficacy of love, and his respect for the forms and ties of society.

It was natural that Tennyson should be concerned with such questions. He grew up during a period of accelerated industrial expansion, when the railway and the steamship were demolishing distances, and production was multiplying rapidly; a time of great wealth for some, and great depression for many; a time when there seemed no limit to possible material progress, and yet, for all the fast growing prosperity of the country as a whole, the nation seemed to many intelligent people to be split into two nations, the rich and the poor, or worse, into a collection of individuals, each regardless of his neighbour, a society

> where there is no longer any Social Idea extant; not so much as the Idea of a common Home, but only of a common overcrowded Lodging house. Where each, isolated, regardless of his neighbour, turned against his neighbour, clutches what he can get, and cries 'Mine!' . . . Where your Priest has no tongue but for platelicking: and your high Guides and Governors cannot guide; but on all hands hear it passionately proclaimed: *Laissez faire*; Leave us alone of *your* guidance, such light is darker than darkness. . . . The Poor perishing, like neglected foundered Draught-Cattle, of Hunger and Overwork; the Rich, still more wretchedly, of Idleness, Satiety, and Overgrowth.[1]

It was a time of much civil unrest, of the growth of the Chartist movement, and of conscious agitation among the workers. It was also a time of acute religious controversy, of the rise of the Oxford movement, and a rapid growth of dissenting sects.

Tennyson could not avoid seeing and feeling these things, and the Shelleyan note of the early poem *Love*, with its cry

> *earth waiteth for thee:*
> *Breathe on thy winged throne, and it shall move*
> *In music and in light o'er land and sea,*

and its image of dying into life 'with the pangs of a new birth', is not repeated. For him the world and its problems were too near, too vivid a reality to be subsumed in the higher reality of the one life. It is true that his response to these problems was, on certain levels, that of the son of a country clergyman with upper-middle-class sympathies, and nothing more; but the *English Idylls* and other such pieces are poems of duty and not of necessity, and cannot be taken as the measure of his mind. In his best poetry he returns continually to the question of the split between science and

[1] Thomas Carlyle, *Sartor Resartus* (1833-8), Book III, Chapter V.

faith, or, in his terms, knowledge and wisdom, seeking a resolution, a greater unity. Shelley had described the situation well:

> The cultivation of those sciences which have enlarged the limits of the empire of man over the external world, has, for want of the poetical faculty, proportionally circumscribed those of the internal world; and man, having enslaved the elements, remains himself a slave . . . the accumulation of the materials of external life exceed the quantity of the power of assimilating them to the internal laws of human nature.[1]

But here Shelley was defending the moral value of poetry, and offering an explanation of the evils of society; the process he analysed as a critic was easily resolved for him in the vision of love unifying all. By the time Tennyson matured, the results of this process seemed to be affecting every aspect of life. Their two great elegies are a measure of the difference: the death of Keats served for Shelley as one more vehicle for the vision that is common to all his best poems; the death of Hallam produced in Tennyson a unique crystallization of his conflicting thoughts and feelings, and *In Memoriam* is the one poem in which he achieves, after bitter struggle, a unified vision.

By 1850, when it was published, he had arranged the 131 lyrics written at odd times, mostly in the 1830s, into a sequence in such a way as to conceal their true chronology and impose an artificial one. The main divisions, he said himself, are marked by the sections which refer to Christmas (xxviii, lxxviii, civ); the lapse of time in the poem is between two and three years, involving the three Christmases after the death of Hallam in September 1833, and ending, apparently, in spring or summer 1836. This internal chronology is carefully arranged to give the reader a sense of time passing;

---

[1] *Shelley's Literary and Philosophical Criticism*, pp. 151, 152, cited in M. H. Abrams, *The Mirror and the Lamp*, Chapter XI, which is an excellent account of the Utilitarian attack on poetry as useless, and the growth of the view that there is a conflict between science and poetry.

THE RHETORIC OF FAITH

there are many allusions to the passing of the seasons, and three sections commemorate the anniversary of Hallam's death. The sections on the Christmases and on the anniversaries are made especially prominent by the repetition of lines carried over from one to another, for instance, 'The time draws near the birth of Christ' (xxviii, civ), and 'Risest thou thus, dim dawn, again' (lxxii, xcix). There are echoes and references back in a number of other sections, and indeed, Tennyson added the present Section xxxix, 'Old warder of these buried bones', after first publication, in order to provide another linkage, in this case with Section ii, 'Old Yew, which graspest at the stones'. He sought to give the poem unity by these means, and to make us read it as a whole,[1] and framed the progress of the theme in a sequence of time.

The main outline of this progress is similar to that in *Adonais*; the poem begins in despair and moves through a period of doubt to a final assertion of faith. It is usual to relate it to a division of the poem into four parts, Sections i-xxx, xxxi-lxxvii, lxxviii-civ, and civ to the end, as Tennyson suggested[2]; but this is to link the internal chronology too closely to the structure. The time scheme is very important in providing a kind of narrative thread which gives a superficial unity to *In Memoriam*, a pattern of sequence. The passage of time over a period of three years also is very important, for the very gradual change from despair to hope, and the difficulty with which it is made, are essential features of the poem. It was natural that Tennyson should pay much attention to the time sequence in order to give a clear and consecutive arrangement to a large collection of lyrics, to create the impression that they are in some sense one long

---

[1] The fictitious chronology conflicts with the true chronology of events on occasion, as for instance in Section xxi, 'I sing to him that rests below', which mentions the grasses on Hallam's grave. This comes before the first Christmas (Section xxviii) after his death, and at this time the body was still in transit from Vienna to Bristol.

[2] Hallam Tennyson, *Alfred Lord Tennyson. A Memoir* (2 vols., 1897), i. 305; see A. C. Bradley, *A Commentary on Tennyson's In Memoriam* (1901), pp. 30ff.

poem, while retaining the individuality of each. But the time sequence is not to be identified with the poem's structure. Seasons and times do not bear an organic relationship to the change of mood, as does the progress from winter to summer in *Adonais*; there is no sense of the one life within us and abroad, and the natural world is separated from the poet. It may seem neutral, it sometimes contradicts his feelings, as in Section xxxviii the spring gives him no pleasure,

> No joy the blowing season gives,
> The herald melodies of spring . . .,

and it may also be hostile, 'red in tooth and claw'; the seasons, the Christmases, the anniversaries, mark his progress to an assertion of faith not by any change in them or any symbolic values they are given, but simply as measures of time.

At the same time, the large amount of natural description in *In Memoriam* is functional and related to the structure in that Tennyson relies on the familiar associations of various kinds of natural scene to embody and reinforce his mood or attitude. Scenes of stillness and beauty are often allied to peaceful moods, scenes of storm or tumult to moods of anguish. The poem tends to oscillate from one to the other in opposed sections or groups of sections, until a final resolution is reached in a love involving the whole world.[1] The beneficent aspects of nature provide images for the poet's times of calmness, as in Section xi, 'Calm is the morn without a sound', where it is the calmness of despair, or Section lxvii, 'When on my bed the moonlight falls', where it is the calmness of true peace, and his times of joy, as in Sections lxxxvi, 'Sweet after showers, ambrosial air', or xci, 'When rosy plumelets tuft the larch'; and the indifferent or hostile aspects of nature afford images for states of pain and doubt as in Sections xv, 'Tonight the winds begin to rise',

---

[1] Contrast *Adonais*, where nature remains constant as a type of eternal beauty, and the oscillation is between the assertions that Adonais is dead, and that he lives.

or lxxii, 'Risest thou thus, dim dawn, again'. In the final reconciliation, the beneficent aspects predominate when 'every thought breaks out a rose', but all are absorbed in the faith that

> *all is well, though faith and form*
> *Be sunder'd in the night of fear;*
> *Well roars the storm to those that hear*
> *A deeper voice across the storm.*

This alternation of moods offers a clue to the structure of the poem as a whole. It is reflected in other groups of images. As in *Adonais* and much Romantic poetry, the most prominent imagery is of light and darkness (warmth and coldness), associated respectively with life, love, faith, infinity, and death, grief, waste, despair. These associations are developed right at the beginning of *In Memoriam* in Section ii, where the 'sullen' yew with its 'dusk' and 'gloom' seems an emblem of the poet's enduring grief,

> *O not for thee the glow, the bloom;*

and again in Section iv, in which he yields his will as 'bondsman to the dark' in the 'frost' of his grief at night, until the morning brings a return of courage,

> *Such clouds of nameless trouble cross*
> *All night below the darken'd eyes*
> *With morning wakes the will, and cries,*
> *'Thou shalt not be the fool of loss'.*

This section illustrates a characteristic technique of the poem; it is on the surface a simple expression of mood, but in the transition from night to day, from a sense of utter loss to a more positive attitude, it adumbrates the movement of the whole. Such hints of recovery contrast with the despair, for instance, of the famous Section vii, where the day brings no relief to his darkness; it is a day without light,

TENNYSON'S *IN MEMORIAM*

> *ghastly through the drizzling rain,*
> *On the bald street breaks the blank day.*

But even in these early sections the light continually breaks through the night of grief, the light that is like love shining on the ship which carries Hallam's remains,

> *Phosphor, bright*
> *As our pure love, through early light*
> *Shall glimmer on the dewy decks;* (ix)

the light that represents the joy of his life with his friend, 'the day of my delight', the glory which seems in retrospect 'the perfect star' (xxiv); the light that has religious associations of peace and comfort,

> *My blessing, like a line of light,*
> *Is on the waters day and night,*
> *And like a beacon guards thee home.* (xvii)

This range of values connected with light gives a special richness to sections like the superb 'Calm is the morn without a sound' (xi), which again is superficially the expression of a mood of calm despair; in it the poet's grief is tempered by the 'deep peace' of an autumn morning, and then, as the description expands, is counterbalanced by it and identified with it. For the peace, which involves the whole world, has a brightness about it in the red leaves, the 'silvery gossamers That twinkle into green and gold', and in the 'still light' shining over all, which seems to conflict with the 'faded leaf', the sense of loss. The echoing word 'calm' is applied to the natural scene, to the poet's own mood, 'If any calm, a calm despair', and to the 'dead calm' in the corpse of Hallam, so that all three seem to share the same quality, and the predominant note of this calm is the bright peace that extends over the world as far as eye can see, so that the imagery counterbalances the overt statement of mood, and the effect of the lyric is one of hope rather than despair. The tendency

THE RHETORIC OF FAITH

through the early sections as they alternate between despair and faint hope, unrest and peace, grief and love, is for hope to predominate, and they culminate in the joy of the first Christmas after Hallam's death, in the assertion of his immortality, and the cry

> *Rise, happy morn, rise, holy morn,*
> *Draw forth the cheerful day from night:*
> *O Father, touch the east, and light*
> *The light that shone when Hope was born.* (xxx)

The sections following this first climax extend the theme of the poem beyond the personal questioning of the beginning to more general problems, and alternate between an avowal of faith in life after death and in renewed friendship with Hallam, and loss of that faith in view of the apparent lack of direction in life when nature is 'so careless of the single life'. Again light and hope predominate over darkness and despair, and the triumph of life is suggested right away,

> *My own dim life should teach me this,*
> *That life shall live for evermore,*
> *Else earth is darkness at the core;* (xxxiv)

but thoughts of Hallam's death return to make him see this 'orb of flame' as little more than 'vacant darkness'. The alternation of mood is beautifully described in Section xxxix, in the image of the yew bursting into flower, 'To thee too comes the golden hour', and passing into gloom again. The poet also needs the assurance of a personal reunion with Hallam in 'that deep dawn behind the tomb', and his hope for this before 'we lose ourselves in light' is set against moments of doubt, when he can only cry, 'Be near me when my light is low', and the life after death seems a twilight, not a dawn,

> *And on the low dark verge of life,*
> *The twilight of eternal day.* (l)

Eventually his doubts and gropings, his fears that he must seem to Hallam 'a growth of cold and night', and his sense at times of being

> *An infant crying in the night,*
> *An infant crying for the light,* (liv)

are resolved in another climax of assertion, in the acceptance of death as a part of life,

> *His inner day can never die,*
> *His night of loss is always there.* (lxvi)

The climax is reached in Sections lxvii-lxxi, all concerned with sleep,[1] for the consolation the poet finds at this stage of his progress is in dreams: in the night, in his sleep, he has the experience of a 'mystic glory', when his crown of thorns is touched into leaf, and Hallam's face appears to him and stills all doubts and troubles.

The feeling of defeat abruptly returns with the day, the second anniversary of the death,

> *Risest thou thus, dim dawn, again,*
> *And howlest issuing out of night . . .?* (lxxii)

The mystic glory of the dream does not sustain the poet in his daily life, and this provides the theme for the following sections, in which the painful thoughts of the greatness Hallam would have achieved, and of how the world 'Is cold to all that might have been', are counterbalanced by the sense of a continuance of his life in Tennyson's:

> *I felt and feel, though left alone,*
> *His being working in mine own.* (lxxxv)

The general tone is softer now, the note of hope much stronger, and the poet learns to accept this life again, and to

---

[1] Cf. Sections iv, xiii, xviii, where sleep is associated with grief and unrest.

cease wishing for some personal contact with the dead; his cry now is for peace,

> *let the fancy fly*
>
> *From belt to belt of crimson seas*
> *On leagues of odour streaming far,*
> *To where in yonder orient star*
> *A hundred spirits whisper 'Peace'.* (lxxxvi)

As he becomes reconciled to life again, he hopes for a spiritual communion with Hallam,

> *Come, beauteous in thine after form,*
> *And like a finer light in light,* (xci)

a communion which is finally granted to him at the culmination of these sections, and when he has achieved the peace of mind necessary to call back 'The spirits from their golden day'. Section xcv describes a summer night when he fell into a kind of trance,

> *And all at once it seem'd at last*
> *The living soul was flash'd on mine.*

He emerges from this trance-like state, which, poetically, lasts all night where he had remained outside the house after a party, only with the dawn, which becomes a symbol of his final achievement of peace, as

> *East and West, without a breath,*
> *Mixt their dim lights, like life and death,*
> *To broaden into boundless day.*

The mixture of life and death in 'boundless day', in an infinite light of joy, peace, blessing, love, which subsumes the darkness, is the theme of the final sections of the poem. These confirm the optimism of Section xcv, in the further dream of a reunion with Hallam in Section ciii, in the poet's full acceptance of life, 'I will not shut me from my kind', in the happiness of the third Christmas, and the 'balmy breath' of the third anniversary of Hallam's death. But they also extend the poet's aspiration beyond a hope for physical or spiritual contact with Hallam to include the unity of all things. The darkness and the light are no longer opposed, but united in a 'stronger faith',

> *And Power was with him in the night,*
> *Which makes the darkness and the light,*
> *And dwells not in the light alone,*
>
> *But in the darkness and the cloud* . . .   (xcvi)

His love is no longer confined to Hallam, but 'sees himself in all he sees', and it is dramatically appropriate that the sections describing the abandonment of his Lincolnshire home (c–ciii) should occur here; for the desertion of the old home with its many associations with Hallam is symbolic of Tennyson's full renewal of life, expressed in his dream of sailing out with his friend towards the 'crimson cloud' that seems to represent a future of harmony and love. The general renewal of life in spring with its gleaming colours and brightness, 'Now dance the lights on lawn and lea', contributes to this final assertion, symbolized again in the union of the evening star, 'Sad Hesper', with the morning star, 'Bright Phosphor', both of them Venus, emblems of love,

> *Sweet Hesper-Phosphor, double name*
> *For what is one, the first, the last,*
> *Thou, like my present and my past,*
> *Thy place is changed: thou art the same.*   (cxxi)

The poem ends with a vision of love, a diffusion of Hallam's presence through all things in a general blessing,

> *Behold, I dream a dream of good,*
> *And mingle all the world with thee:*   (cxxix)

and Tennyson is finally at peace with a life in which Hallam's being gives beauty equally to light and darkness,

> *Thou standest in the rising sun,*
> *And in the setting thou art fair.* (cxxx)

Other threads of imagery support this general pattern. The battle of light and darkness, love and despair, is reflected in oppositions between images of music, harmony, peace, and images of storm and tumult; between images of ascent and images of descent; and between images of death, represented particularly in the word 'dust',

> *Man dies; nor is there hope in dust . . .* (xxxv)

> *And Time, a maniac scattering dust . . .* (l)

> *I stretch lame hands of faith, and grope,*
> *And gather dust and chaff . . . ,* (lv)

and images of life, the flowering of nature, and birth,

> *the songs, the stirring air,*
> *The life re-orient out of dust . . .* (cxvi)

The poet's progress from despair through a recovery of faith in Hallam's immortality, and belief that their love will allow a personal reunion,

> *O Love, thy province were not large,*
> *A bounded field, nor stretching far . . . ,* (xlvi)

to a faith in a spiritual reunion, and the extension of his personal love to involve the universe,

> *My love involves the love before;*
> *My love is vaster passion now;*
> *Though mix'd with God and Nature thou,*
> *I seem to love thee more and more;* (cxxx)

this progress is reflected in the image of a journey, and also, in a different way, in imagery of the sea. The death of Hallam left Tennyson alone to 'wander, often falling lame' on a cheerless path of life; his grief is expressed in the description of himself as a lonely voyager, 'Still onwards winds the dreary way . . .' (xxvi), 'With weary steps I loiter on . . .' (xxxviii), separated from his companion,

> *My paths are in the fields I know,*
> *And thine in undiscover'd lands.* (xl)

But this sense of separation is gradually replaced by the sense that 'nothing walks with aimless feet', by dreams of a reunion with Hallam, of a goal for his journey,

> *Arrive at last the blessed goal,*
> *And he that died in Holy Land*
> *Would reach us out the shining hand,*
> *And take us as a single soul.* (lxxxiv)

This culminates in the break with his old life in his departure from home (c–cii), and vision of the future as a journey forward with Hallam to a rosy future. Here the image of the journey is linked with the image of the sea, in the poet's dream of sailing out across the ocean

> *toward a crimson cloud*
> *That landlike slept along the deep.* (ciii)

The sea is introduced naturally at the beginning of the poem as carrying the ship that bears the body of Hallam back to England; it is a vast and uncertain area, a place of calm and tempest, of fear and loneliness, 'placid ocean-plains' and 'roaring wells' that may drown Hallam 'fathom-deep in brine'; above all it represents the unexplored space away from home, as in

> *The moanings of the homeless sea . . .* (xxxv)

THE RHETORIC OF FAITH

So by an easy transition the sea comes to be an image for the uncertain future that the poet must face, where for a time he sees alternately

> *shoals of pucker'd faces drive;*
> *Dark bulks that tumble half alive,*
> *And lazy lengths on boundless shores* .. (lxx)

and brighter visions of peace and certainty,

> *From belt to belt of crimson seas*
> *On leagues of odours streaming far,*
> *To where in yonder orient star,*
> *A hundred spirits whisper 'Peace'.* (lxxxvi)

But finally security is assured in his vision of sailing with Hallam, in a harmony of sound, towards a bright land (Section ciii), and in the faith that whatever storms may come in that sea, as

> *No doubt vast eddies in the flood*
> *Of onward time shall yet be made . . .,*
> (cxxviii)

the future belongs to love and goodness. So in a sense the poet's journey ends, although time still stretches, an unknown sea, before him, in this assurance that all is well; and he says

> *But in my spirit will I dwell,*
> *And dream my dream and hold it true,*
> (cxxiii)

for he is strengthened by a sense of universal love,

> *Abiding with me till I sail*
> *To seek thee on the mystic deeps.* (cxxv)

One other important thread of imagery relates to the home,

the family and household. At the beginning of the poem the poet compares himself to a girl who has lost her lover (Section vi), or a man whose mistress has deserted him,

> *And all the place is dark, and all*
> *The chambers emptied of delight;* (viii)

or he likens himself to a widower or widow (Sections xiii, xvii), or to servants or children in a house where the master has just died (Section xx). He thus suggests both his intimacy with the dead Hallam and his sense of utter desertion, that 'all is dark where thou art not'. In his initial grief he feels alienated from society, and asks only for 'Silence, till I be silent too'; this sense of the meaninglessness of life is expressed most poignantly in Section vii, in his visit to the 'Dark house' where Hallam lived,

> *far away*
> *The noise of life begins again,*
> *And ghastly through the drizzling rain*
> *On the bald street breaks the blank day.*

The poet's recovery from this state of despair has begun by Section xxx, when the festivity of the first Christmas after Hallam's death brings joy to him, and communion with others. Now the image of widowhood or uncompleted love gives way to the image of marriage or the continuance of love. At first this is expressed as a hope,

> *Could we forget the widow'd hour*
> *And look on Spirits breathed away,*
> *As on a maiden in the day*
> *When first she wears her orange-flower!* (xl)

Then he learns to make a bride of his sorrow (Section lix), and to think of himself not as widowed but as still loving Hallam, like a girl

> *whose heart is set*
> *On one whose rank exceeds her own.* (lx)

So through the contemplation of the daily life they might have led had Hallam lived, Tennyson comes to feel the need of human affection, becomes 'kindly with my kind', and cannot live solely in thoughts of what might have been,

> *My heart, though widow'd, may not rest*
> *Quite in the love of what is gone,*
> *But seeks to beat in time with one*
> *That warms another living breast.* (lxxxv)

It is appropriate that the climactic vision of spiritual communion with Hallam takes place by his home, and after the 'genial warmth' of a summer party, for the full renewal of his sense of kinship with Hallam corresponds with a full resumption of the ordinary relationships of life. His love expands to include the universe, 'He sees himself in all he sees', and he thinks of his dead friend and himself as 'Two partners of a married life' (Section xcvii), whose love 'has never past away'. The removal from his old home brings the final break with the 'bond of dying use', and an affirmation of a return to life, 'I will not shut me from my kind'; released from grief, he is enabled to revisit Hallam's house with a light heart,

> *Doors, where my heart was used to beat*
> *So quickly, not as one that weeps*
> *I come once more; the city sleeps:*
> *I smell the meadow in the street;*
>
> *I hear the chirp of birds; I see*
> *Betwixt the black fronts long-withdrawn*
> *A light-blue lane of early dawn,*
> *And think of early days and thee . . .* (cxix)

The strength of *In Memoriam* lies in this finely organized progress, marked by three climaxes in Sections xxx, lxvii-lxx, and xcv, from darkness to light, from despair to the assertion that 'all is well'. The power of this reassurance commended

TENNYSON'S *IN MEMORIAM*

it to the large Victorian public which found consolation and wisdom in the poem at a time when the foundations of the Christian faith seemed to be threatened by the advance of science and the new evolutionary theories explaining the origin of life.[1] *In Memoriam* was valued as a religious document, for the teaching it contained,[2] and when, in the present century, it fell out of favour, the reaction was not against the poem as poem, but against what now appeared a very inadequate teaching, 'Tennyson was a fool to try to write a poetry which would teach the Ideal', or a very inadequate faith,

> It is not religious because of the quality of its faith, but because of the quality of its doubt. Its faith is a poor thing, but its doubt is a very intense experience.[3]

The truth is that the poem does not teach at all; it seemed to do so to its Victorian audience because it identified their doubts, presented simply and memorably what they were vaguely feeling, and saved them the trouble of thinking things out; it offered the comfort of its assertion as a resting place for troubled minds. Its Christian faith may be a poor thing, but it is an adjunct of the central experience expressed in the poem, which is truly religious only in the widest sense, the sense in which, for instance, *Adonais* is a religious work;

[1] For an account of the influence of Charles Lyell's *Principles of Geology* (1830-3), which put forward a 'theory of natural laws operating ruthlessly throughout the earth's history', on Tennyson during the composition of *In Memoriam*, see Eleanor B. Mattes, *In Memoriam: The Way of a Soul* (New York, 1951) pp. 49-63, and cf. Basil Willey, *More Nineteenth-Century Studies* (1956), pp. 84ff.
[2] See A. C. Bradley, *A Commentary on Tennyson's In Memoriam* (1901), p. 36, 'It is a fashion at present to ascribe the great popularity of *In Memoriam* entirely to the "teaching" contained in it. . . .'
[3] W. H. Auden, *A Selection from the Poems of Alfred, Lord Tennyson* (New York, 1944), p. xix; T. S. Eliot, *Essays Ancient and Modern* (1936), p. 187. In his essay on *In Memoriam* in *All in Due Time* (1955), pp. 130-9, Humphry House sees the 'true development' of the poem as lying 'less in the assertions of the power of love . . . than in those moments of achieved happiness and hope, in which the optimistic evolutionary philosophy is not described, but simply taken for granted, as providing the setting and the mode of thought'.

that is, in coming to terms with death by recognizing an enduring value in the harmony of love, or other human ideals, and affirming immortality as a sign of man's greatness in the face of apparent oblivion.

There is no intellectual advance in *In Memoriam*; the dichotomy between knowledge and wisdom, science and faith, is present at the beginning and the end, and is summed up in the prologue added in 1849,

> *We have but faith: we cannot know;*
> *For knowledge is of things we see;*
> *And yet we trust it comes from thee,*
> *A beam in darkness: let it grow.*
>
> *Let knowledge grow from more to more,*
> *But more of reverence in us dwell . . .*

In Memoriam reflects problems which worried Tennyson and many other Victorians, but it does not solve them: it overrides them, resolves them into a higher unity, in the intensity of the poet's vision of love. The poem's progress is an emotional one, and the triumphant assertion which finally replaces the despair of grief corresponds in many ways to Shelley's assertion in *Adonais*; it is a love and benediction diffused through the universe,

> *Thy voice is on the rolling air;*
> *I hear thee where the waters run;*
> *Thou standest in the rising sun,*
> *And in the setting thou art fair.* (cxxx)

There is no essential connexion between this and a Christian faith. The problem which Tennyson frequently states in the poem, of the antagonism between science and religion, in a world in which spiritual progress was lagging behind material progress, and the consequent difficulty of accepting Christian beliefs, was a matter of great concern to him. He desired to have the certainty that human life was advancing towards

TENNYSON'S *IN MEMORIAM*

some goal; he wanted to believe, to christianize his love for Hallam. But he found no answer to the problem, and the cry that all is well in the world stems not from a renewal of faith in God, but from a renewal of faith in love. To concentrate on the former, and think of *In Memoriam* as a religious poem in a Christian sense or as a discussion of contemporary problems, is sure to bring disappointment; its value as a poem resides in its quality as a vision of love, which ultimately transcends the poet's difficulties with both science and faith.

III

Most of the contemporary reviewers of *In Memoriam* praised its theology, but one, in the *English Review*, accused the poet of blasphemy, and suggested that he really had no faith at all, or was '*an exclusive worshipper of the beautiful*'.[1] This was unkind but perceptive; there is no genuine integration of his troubled faith with the vision of love. Shelley's vision of a beneficent unity transcends life's 'unquiet dream', and absorbs the universe in the 'beauty in which all things work and move'; but Tennyson's dream of mingling 'all the world with thee', i.e. Hallam, transcends without absorbing those questions he wanted to answer, without explaining life's problems. His response to these problems now seems inadequate, not his response to Hallam's death: the inadequacy lies not in his failure to be profound, to see beyond his time and society, but in the lack of integration. It is seen in a failure of his language to carry conviction. The rhetoric of assertion is appropriate only to the true visionary utterance, for instance to the joy of his sense of renewed communion with Hallam, as in 'Love is and was my Lord and King', and the vocabulary of love, sorrow, despair, and trust, fortified as it is by the patterns of imagery, suits admirably the personal progress in the poem. But the rhetorical vocabulary used in the discussion of general problems now seems empty and barren, for it is unsupported by the central imagery or

[1] Edgar Finley Shannon, Junior, *Tennyson and the Reviewers*, pp. 149-51.

the central theme of the poem, and is not subsumed, as Tennyson wanted it to be, in a total vision. The conflicts between Nature and God, Science and Faith, Knowledge and Wisdom, remain abstract, and these terms have no real poetic life in themselves, but only as symbols of the poet's suffering, his sense of emptiness and futility in his grief at the loss of Hallam, or as a measure of the degree to which the vision of love is earned.[1] And the vocabulary of the solutions he suggests or hopes for, the wish for human progress in terms of noble manners, social truth, the 'grand old name of gentleman', and for a reconciliation between Nature and God in 'toil co-operant to an end', or 'the closing cycle rich in good', remains hollow and nerveless.

It was a sign of his times that Tennyson was no longer able, as Shelley had been, to make a single, inclusive response to life. His vision is more limited, and his prospect of love does not embrace society (where justice seems more real and important to him), and trembles before a natural world that reveals no certain order. The vision of love, however, remains genuine, and is not contaminated, turned into something else, by the other elements in *In Memoriam*, and it is perhaps as well that the reconciliation Tennyson desired and attempted was not achieved. Browning, his contemporary, did not attempt to make this reconciliation. A vision of love is still at the centre of his best poetry,[2] but it is concentrated

---

[1] As, for example, the image of a purposeless and godless Nature 'red in tooth and claw' (lvi) reflects the despair of grief, and is replaced by the image of a purposive Nature, linked with God, as the poet's despair is overcome (cf. Section cxviii, and the ideal image of Hallam as one in whom 'God and Nature met in light' in Section cxi).

[2] Since this book was written Robert Langbaum's *The Poetry of Experience* (1957) has appeared, a very fine analysis of the emergence of the dramatic monologue as a characteristic form of modern poetry; in it Browning's poetry is sympathetically appraised. Mr Langbaum sees the modern world as one 'where there is no valid moral principle for connecting the events, where we are left with perspectives toward the events', and 'can adopt the perspective of only one character at a time' (p. 226): so he argues that literature which takes account of the modern situation 'approximates the dramatic monologue', in which, 'through seeing what the speaker sees within the limits of his perspective, . . . we apprehend his total life and therefore our own' (p. 205); for there

in the individual, in 'the development of a soul: little else is worth study. I, at least, always thought so.'[1] The climax of this development, as in Shelley's and Tennyson's vision, is a dying into life, represented for instance in the passion of *Saul*,

> *By the pain-throb, triumphantly winning intensified bliss,*
> *And the next world's reward and repose, by the struggle in this:*

or again, it is represented dramatically in *In a Balcony*, where by acknowledging their love for each other, Norbert and Constance go to certain death, but only thus fulfil their lives, welcoming their state as 'past harm . . . On the breast of God'.

The struggle of the soul towards its full development is not portrayed solely in terms of a fulfilment of love, but the poems which present it in other terms, the poems on artists, on men who lived before the time of Christ, pagans or a pagan world, and on various religious figures, have a bearing on the vision of love. For if Browning did not attempt to reconcile the vision with a solution to religious and social problems, he at least wanted to christianize it. These poems reflect the

is no 'publicly accepted moral and emotional Truth, there are only perspectives toward it—those partial meanings which individuals may get a glimpse of at particular moments' (p. 137). The 'meaning' of *Bishop Blougram's Apology* then becomes 'the strength of will and intellect Blougram reveals through his manipulation of the Christian argument' (p. 207), and of *Childe Roland* Mr Langbaum says, 'The triumph in the end I would call existential rather than moral' (p. 194). This is a very different account of these poems from the one outlined in the present study, but the two views are perhaps complementary, and are both based on a recognition of the disappearance of absolute standards. Mr Langbaum is concerned with the nature and achievement of modern poetry (what he calls 'poetry of experience' is allied to what I have called poetry of conflict), and stresses Browning's contribution to a poetry of limited perspectives; I am concerned with the continuance of the Romantic vision, and have stressed rather his belief that 'Art remains the one way possible of speaking truth', his assertion, as voiced by the Pope, whom Mr Langbaum calls 'authoritative', in *The Ring and the Book*,

> *let love be so,*
> *Unlimited in its self-sacrifice,*
> *Then is the tale true and God shows complete.*

[1] Preface to *Sordello* (1863).

difficulties and uncertainties of his theology. Some of them preach the doctrine that 'What's come to perfection perishes'; so Gothic art, the unfinished work, is praised and the finality of classical art disparaged, life being a toil towards the serenity of heaven,

> *Things learned on earth, we shall practise in heaven.*

The perfect representation of the beauty of Lucrezia in his paintings leaves Andrea del Sarto dissatisfied,

> *Ah, but a man's reach should exceed his grasp,*
> *Or what's a heaven for?*

Again in *Cleon* a Greek artist is imagined, who has achieved absolute success in all his work, poetry, painting, music, sculpture, but feels as he grows old that his capability for joy increases as his physical powers diminish, and wishes that there were another life in which he could fulfil his yearning, 'Unlimited in capability For joy'. Linked with these are portraits of men like the grammarian in *A Grammarian's Funeral* who set themselves some great task and failed to achieve it, or Rabbi Ben Ezra, who also has no great achievement to show, but is certain that

> *Shall life succeed in that it seems to fail:*
> *What I aspired to be*
> *And was not comforts me.*

Other poems seem to contradict this doctrine. The most notable perhaps is *Bishop Blougram's Apology*, in which poor Gigadibs, the literary gentleman, who keeps his ideals, wants in his beliefs as in everything to be 'whole and sole' himself, receives such a mental drubbing. Gigadibs refuses Christianity because of his doubts, and the bishop, who has accepted doubt as a necessary part of his faith, triumphs over him not on moral grounds, but partly because he can claim to have fought his doubts,

BROWNING'S *MEN AND WOMEN*

> *No, when the fight begins within himself,*
> *A man's worth something. God stoops o'er his head,*
> *Satan looks up between his feet—both tug—*
> *He's left himself i'the middle: the soul wakes*
> *And grows. Prolong that battle through his life!*
> *Never leave growing till the life to come!*

and partly because he is so successful in his career, has achieved material wealth and greatness,

> *I act for, talk for, live for this world now,*
> *As this world prizes action, life and talk...*
> *Success I recognize and compliment.*

The bishop proclaims that a man should struggle to fulfil himself, 'I live my life here; yours you dare not live', and places the value of life in that struggle, in continual growth. Yet he has achieved success in this life just as Cleon had, and opposes his ideal realized to the ideal of Gigadibs,

> *your grand simple life,*
> *Of which you will not realize one jot.*
> *I am much, you are nothing; you would be all,*
> *I would be merely much: you beat me there.*

It is difficult to see what struggle is left for the bishop, or what further growth is possible; he has not a pure faith, but he has accepted the 'Doubts at the very bases of my soul' as part of the state of things, and cannot fight them directly. His way of answering them is 'To mould life as we choose it', to 'have a life to show' as a kind of assertion of the faith he wants, and the life he has to show is his rise to power in his career in the church. It is through this that he has carried out his principle,

> *It is the idea, the feeling and the love,*
> *God means mankind should strive for and show forth*
> *Whatever be the process to that end.*

THE RHETORIC OF FAITH

What really matters for the bishop is that the individual should realize his potentialities to the full, 'whatever be the process to that end', and he sneers at Gigadibs for not doing so; as he says then,

> *How one acts*
> *Is, both of us agree, our chief concern.*

There is nothing essentially Christian about this attitude to life, and the bishop's complacency matches ill with the dissatisfaction of Cleon, who certainly realized his capabilities to the full, and that of Andrea del Sarto, who seems to be morally reproved, and feels himself a failure in spite of having followed the bishop's advice. Cleon had the misfortune to live before the time of Christ, but there is no qualitative difference between his success and that of Blougram; Andrea del Sarto is involved in a moral difficulty, and has a guilty conscience over the wrong he did to Francis I, but otherwise there is again no qualitative difference between his way of adapting himself to life and that of the bishop—unless it is that he chose the wrong woman. The contradiction between the bishop's principle, which is put most succinctly in *The Statue and the Bust*,

> *Let a man contend to the uttermost*
> *For his life's set prize, be it what it will!*

and the plea that 'a man's reach should exceed his grasp' is not resolved in these poems.

The contradiction is not really resolved at all. The attainment of 'life's set prize' means for Cleon discouragement and horror at the thought of death, the thought that his growing capability for joy must come to an end; heaven as he imagines it would be the continuance in perfection of the best of earthly life, and this is the characteristic conception in Browning's verse, the picture suggested in *The Last Ride Together*,

> *What if heaven be that, fair and strong*
> *At life's best, with our eyes upturned*

> *Whither life's flower is first discerned,*
> *We, fixed so, ever should so abide?*
> *What if we still ride on, we two*
> *With life for ever old yet new,*
> *Changed not in kind but in degree,*
> *The instant made eternity . . .*

It is difficult to imagine how Andrea del Sarto would fit in to such an after-life, or what exercise there would be for Bishop Blougram's talents in heaven. The pattern is clear for those who aspire to some great work on earth and fail to achieve it, for heaven can be the completion of that aspiration,

> *God's task to make the heavenly period*
> *Perfect the earthen.*

It seems to be clear too for those who fail to contend at all, thereby sin and are condemned. But those who achieve their set prize in this life are not so easily provided for.

If it be argued that there is still something for Andrea del Sarto and Blougram to find in heaven as a completion of their lives, one way remains in which the soul can be fulfilled in this world, through love between man and woman. *By the Fire-Side* describes the moment when two lovers first acknowledge their love, and give themselves to one another, and moralizes on this,

> *How the world is made for each of us!*
> *How all we perceive and know in it*
> *Tends to some moment's product thus,*
> *When a soul declares itself—to wit,*
> *By its fruit, the thing it does! . . .*
>
> *I am named and known by that moment's feat;*
> *There took my station and degree;*
> *So grew my own small life complete . . .*

The completion of love is a symbol of Browning's heaven, the heaven that Saul attains, 'a Man like to me, Thou shalt love and be loved by, forever'. A supreme value is put in these poems on the struggle of a man to realize himself, and the one certain way in which that realization can be made concrete and gain general assent regarding its value, is in terms of love. The poems may say that it does not matter how a 'soul declares itself', whether by hate or love, but in fact, love is almost the only valid symbol of the completion of the soul; *Bishop Blougram's Apology*, *Andrea del Sarto* and other poems reflect the difficulties in which the poet becomes involved when he deals with other kinds of human achievement, and their relation to heaven. The centre of his faith is in this world, the 'wild joys of living', of which the next seems to be at worst a copy, at best a completion; and Browning's heaven might be described as a symbol of the completion of love. The love poems are central in Browning's work because they present the most unambiguous and loftiest conception of the struggle and fulfilment of the individual.

Half of the poems in *Men and Women*, Browning's finest collection, are love-poems. Most celebrate in some way the completion of love, but a few condemn those who fail to fulfil their love (*The Statue and the Bust*), or deal with unrequited love (*In a Year*), or a love that is insufficient, the love of *Two in the Campagna*. There is no predominant imagery in these poems; the natural world with its exuberant life, 'Such primal naked forms of flowers', is a recurring point of reference for the possibilities in man's life, and sometimes becomes symbolic, as in *By the Fire-Side*, where the 'powers at play' in the forest are involved with the fruition of the speaker's love, and in *Fra Lippo Lippi*, where the flowers of the song represent the life from which the painter has been cut off since he was a child,

> *Flower o' the broom,*
> *Take away love, and our earth is a tomb!*

The most common image is of light and darkness, as in so much Romantic poetry, the 'new light and new life' that comes to Saul, or the 'one blaze About me and within me' which is the culmination of love for Constance in *In a Balcony*. Light is an image for the moment of release, the completion of the soul, the perfection of love,

> *As night shows where her one moon is,*
> *A hand's-breadth of pure light and bliss,*
> *So life's night gives my lady birth*
> *And my eyes hold her! What is worth*
> *The rest of heaven, the rest of earth?*

But these are not recurrent images developed into symbols of a universal harmony, as in Shelley's poetry, and, to a lesser degree, in *In Memoriam*. Browning's vision has to be created freshly in each poem because it is limited to the individual and does not seek to embrace all humanity. However boldly he rejected Victorian morality in sexual matters, he was at one with his age in putting a high value on the man who strives 'to the uttermost For his life's set prize': his poetry reflects the anarchical principles on which the prosperous new aristocracy of commerce flourished during the later nineteenth century, those mysterious economic laws, laws of supply and demand, which act independently of mankind.

Browning's men and women are characters from an anarchical society; they exist for themselves. The vision of love has dwindled from a promise of harmony for everyone to a hope of salvation for the individual. It is still a noble vision, for the reward of those who strive is a spiritual fulfilment, an ultimate peace and harmony, the perfection of love, or its continued perfection in heaven. Instead of an overall pattern of imagery embodying or sustaining the vision, Browning creates a series of figures who are all either undergoing a crisis in which they must choose whether to fulfil themselves or not, or reflecting on the decision they have made, or they are being examined in the light of a possible fulfilment. The figures are the images embodying the vision. They exist for themselves inasmuch as the problem of fulfilment is different for every individual, but at the same time they exist only in relation to that problem.

It is interesting that the grandest, simplest and least equivocal way of fulfilment, that of love, breaks down the isolation of the individual. Love is a relationship between two or more people. In many poems it is seen from the point of view of one partner in the relationship, as notably in *By the Fire-Side*, in which the sense of a mutual affirmation described in the early part of the poem, that 'two lives join', almost disappears towards the end: there the speaker celebrates his own achievement, 'I am named and known by that moment's feat'. The poems of unrequited love are also of this kind, but the position of those who have given their love to one who does not return it remains uncertain; this is the one area of life in which the fulfilment of self depends on another person. Some may cry, with James Lee's wife,

> *If you loved only what were worth your love,*
> *Love were clear gain, and wholly well for you;*

or the answer may be that love is best anyway,

> *My whole life long I learned to love.*
> *This hour my utmost art I prove*
> *And speak my passion—heaven or hell?*
> *She will not give me heaven? 'Tis well!*
> *Lose who may—I still can say,*
> *Those who win heaven, blest are they!*

The grand culmination of Browning's vision is the winning of heaven, the achievement of the 'mutual flame', the dying into life celebrated in *In a Balcony*,

> *Feel my heart; let it die against your own.*

Love is supreme because it is a release of the self into a greater harmony; Norbert describes his avowal of his long suppressed love for Constance thus:

BROWNING'S *MEN AND WOMEN*

> *I resume*
> *Life after death, (it is no less than life,*
> *After such long unlovely labouring days)*
> *And liberate to beauty life's great need*
> *O' the beautiful . . .*

It is appropriate that the opening poem in *Men and Women* should proclaim the value of love above everything else in life:

> *Earth's returns*
> *For whole centuries of folly, noise and sin!*
> *Shut them in*
> *With their triumphs and their glories and the rest!*
> *Love is best.*

Browning's verse is often criticized for its easy optimism, for presenting an inadequate response to life. As in Tennyson's *In Memoriam*, the inadequacy lies in a lack of integration, and is revealed in the failure of his language to carry conviction. The rhetoric of assertion is appropriate to the fulfilment of love, to the passages cited in the last paragraph for instance, since love is a fitting and universal symbol of life, blessing, harmony and beauty. But Browning attaches a similar kind of assertive vocabulary to other kinds of fulfilment, the worldly success of the hypocritical Blougram, and to failure, failure in love, failure to win worldly success, or that failure represented by a dull perfection, the artistry of Andrea del Sarto. He seems to escape from the profound disquiet at the heart of these poems into generalizations that all is really for the best, and thus to evade the dramatic issues raised in them with assertions that often remain empty rhetoric,

> *That what began best can't end worst.*

The contradictions noted earlier reflect this lack of integration; the simple assertion of a beneficent overall pattern does not correspond to the picture of life represented in the poems, and is unsupported by it. Like Tennyson, Browning did not achieve a unifying vision; Tennyson attempted to do so, but failed to reconcile the diverse elements of his experience, while Browning sought to impose an inadequate formula on his. But if they reflect the decline of the vision of love and the beginnings of a reduction of its vocabulary of assertion to mere rhetoric, they have their greatness: their vision, though limited, is noble and valid, and their response to life much less simple than the rhetoric by which they are often judged would suggest.

[7]

THE VANITY OF RHETORIC

Matthew Arnold's poetry and James Thomson's
The City of Dreadful Night

I

IF for Browning and Tennyson the vision of love diminished in scope, at least it remained a vision which might possibly integrate the universe for them. In *Men and Women* and *In Memoriam* the journey of life still has as its goal a triumph over death; this is not Wordsworth's grand universal

> *feeling of life endless, the great thought*
> *By which we live, Infinity and God,*

but rather a reunion with the best there has been in this life in a glory symbolized by the image of light. One of the finest poems in *Men and Women* evokes the imaginary pilgrimage of Childe Roland, his 'world-wide wandering' in search of the mysterious dark tower, and brings to life its last stages; he travels through a nightmarish landscape as the night closes round him, until the last gleam of the sunset reveals that he has reached his destination, the turret 'blind as the fool's heart'. It is death that lies in wait for him there, and at the last moment he hears the names of all who have travelled on his quest before, 'all the lost adventurers my peers', and sees them ranged along the hillside, 'in a sheet of flame I saw them and I knew them', but still undaunted, sets the horn to his lips. In the quest he was bound to fail like all the others, 'just to fail as they, seemed best'; the important thing is to fare forward boldly on the journey of life; so the noise and

THE VANITY OF RHETORIC

light at the end, the sound like a bell tolling, and the sheet of flame, have a dual quality—they are both a warning of death, and a signal of triumph. At the moment of death he is reunited with his dead companions. Tennyson's journey in *In Memoriam* also culminates in his reunion with Hallam, in a vision of the two of them sailing out across a sea, the sea of infinity perhaps, in company with maidens who seem to represent 'what is wise and good And graceful'; the ship is accompanied by music, and its destination is a glow of light that looks like land, an ultimate rest:

> And while the wind began to sweep
> A music out of sheet and shroud,
> We steer'd her toward a crimson cloud
> That landlike slept along the deep.

The central image in Matthew Arnold's poetry is that of the journey of life, with its attendant images of the river as a type of the passage of time, and the sea, representing both man's experience and the 'Infinite sea' into which the river of life flows. But as the Romantic vision of love suffered a change in the poetry of Tennyson and Browning, so the nature of the journey is very different in Arnold's verse. *The Prelude* ends with an ascent of the soul to spiritual grandeur, a vision of the one life in the universe, and a triumph over that sea of experience through which the poet has voyaged; for Tennyson and Browning there was still a glow of light, a reunion, a promise of life at the finish; but the journey in Arnold's poetry has no goal, or only the vaguest hope of a goal. It is a blind journey towards no fulfilment,

> what was before us we know not,
> And we know not what shall succeed.

There is a chance that peace may await man at the end,

> Haply the river of Time . . .
> May acquire, if not the calm

MATTHEW ARNOLD'S POETRY

> *Of its early mountainous shore,*
> *Yet a solemn peace of its own,*

and bring to us 'Murmurs and scents of the infinite sea'. Sometimes too, on the 'darkling plain' of existence, a man may have a momentary sense of purpose in life, when, during a 'lull in the hot race' in which he is involved,

> *he thinks he knows*
> *The hills where his life rose,*
> *And the sea where it goes.*

In general however, life seems to lead nowhere, to have no pattern,

> *And we shall sink in the impossible strife*
> *And be astray for ever.*

The vision has disintegrated, and there is no harmony, no unity. Human beings are islands for ever separated by 'The unplumb'd salt estranging sea'; or pieces of driftwood aimlessly wandering, meeting and parting again. Even love cannot break down this isolation, but at most can offer a cry of anguish, 'Ah love, let us be true To one another' to set against the 'turbid ebb and flow Of human misery', but not to compensate for it with a prospect of harmony, an overriding vision. The long poems reflect this disintegration. Empedocles; exiled, seeks relief from his isolation in suicide. The wanderings of Sohrab and Rustum in search of each other end in their meeting as opponents in single combat, and Rustum kills the son he refused to recognize. Tristram, doomed by the accidental drinking of a potion to love Iseult of Ireland all his life, is shown at the point of death; she escapes from the court of King Marc, her husband, to return and die with him, and they who were 'ununited' while they lived are buried side by side. Tristram's widow is left in her isolation like one 'dying in a mask of youth', condemned to suffer

THE VANITY OF RHETORIC

> *the gradual furnace of the world,*
> *In whose hot air our spirits are upcurl'd*
> *Until they crumble, or else grow like steel—*
> *Which kills us in the bloom, the youth, the spring—*
> *Which leaves the fierce necessity to feel,*
> *And takes away the power.*

In *Balder Dead* the journey of Hermod to Hela's realm in an attempt to win back the best-loved of the gods proves unsuccessful; the malice of Lok is strong enough to defeat the love of the rest of the world, and bring to nothing the otherwise universal desire that Balder should be restored to heaven. All these poems deal with the death of a figure who is in some way an emblem of disintegration, of those

> *Poor fragments of a broken world*
> *On which men pitch their tent;*

by the accidents of fate Rustum and Tristram are each debarred from union, except in death, with the one person they love above all others in the world; Empedocles is banished by the people he has loved, and there is one to contrive the death of Balder, the most universally beloved of the gods.

A faint assertion of hope breaks through in these poems. Empedocles feels that he will not 'die wholly'; Sohrab dies prophesying that Rustum will find peace, and Tristram has a kind of happiness in his death; and Balder calls on Hermod not to mourn for him, as he offers the prospect of a new heaven remote as yet in time, and far away to the south, which will be more suited to a 'spirit mild', and to

> *a seed of man preserved,*
> *Who then shall live in peace, as now at war.*

The strength of the longer poems, as indicated in Arnold's choice of theme, lies in their depiction of man's isolation from his fellows, their view of man's course in life as that of a 'foil'd circuitous wanderer' like the river Oxus. The most powerful image for the goal of man's journey is that of the sea, the 'luminous home of waters', often associated with the sky and stars, as objects of stability and peace; but significantly, this is an image of rest as such, and is not developed into a symbol of renewed life and love. Generally it remains a hope for man

> *Still bent to make some port he knows not where,*
> *Still standing for some false impossible shore,*

rather than a promise; and as this passage suggests, the sea is in any case an ambiguous image in Arnold's poetry. Is the infinite sea going to provide a repetition of man's experience on the sea of life? It is worth noting the contrast between the use of the sea-image in the poetry of Arnold, and that of Wordsworth and Tennyson—for Arnold life is imaged as a sea, or a river flowing into a sea that is endless, without shores; but in *The Prelude* Wordsworth conquers and rises above the sea of human experience in his ascent of the mountain, and in *In Memoriam* Tennyson's vision is of sailing out together with Hallam on the sea of infinity towards a promise of land. In Arnold's verse it is simply an endless ocean in which the river of life loses itself.

His poetry makes its main impact not in terms of a possible outcome of man's journey, or an acceptance of life with a fearless resignation which may meet approval

> *in His eye,*
> *To whom each moment in its race,*
> *Crowd as we will its neutral space,*
> *Is but a quiet watershed*
> *Whence, equally, the seas of life and death are fed.*

The dominant picture is that presented in *A Summer Night*, of man either imprisoned or sailing in a storm-swept sea driven by 'despotic' winds at the whim of fate, or that of *Dover Beach* with its passionate cry that the world

THE VANITY OF RHETORIC

> *Hath really neither joy, nor love, nor light,*
> *Nor certitude, nor peace, nor help for pain.*

The certitude Arnold could not find in a vision of the future he found in some measure by looking back to the past, or within himself to what he called the buried self. The vocabulary of assertion, which these lines briefly catalogue and reject as meaningless, is restored in relation to the past, which takes on a nostalgic glow in comparison with his own 'iron age'.

This is seen in his peculiar, wistful attitude towards the Romantic poets; his celebration of Goethe as one who took refuge from the world in the truth of art; of Obermann as one who escaped into the natural world to hide

> *thy head*
> *From the fierce tempest of thine age;*

and of Wordsworth as a poet who put aside 'The cloud of mortal destiny' by averting his eyes from 'half of human fate'. Arnold envied them for the peace they attained,

> *Too fast we live, too much are tried,*
> *Too harass'd, to attain*
> *Wordsworth's sweet calm, or Goethe's wide*
> *And luminous view to gain.*

But as he could not share their vision, he remained insensitive to it, and mistook it for blindness or an averting of the eyes; for him no integration was possible, no bright ending to the nightmare journey,

> *As, charter'd by some unknown Powers,*
> *We stem across the sea of life by night.*

One way out lay in the continuance of the journey for ever, and in *The Scholar-Gipsy* Arnold recreated the figure of a student reported to have left Oxford University in the seventeenth century to live and wander with gipsies: he made one most significant change from his source material, as he himself cited it, for while in Glanvil's *Vanity of Dogmatizing* the student is reported to have intended to return to his usual life after a time, in the poem he is imagined as continuing to roam in his 'glad perennial youth'. Arnold's nostalgic view of the past as a time of innocence and gaiety, when 'life ran gaily as the sparkling Thames' is set against his sense of the

> *strange disease of modern life,*
> *With its sick hurry, its divided aims.*

The scholar-gipsy, in abandoning ordinary life to wander in the woods and fields, is similar to the Romantic poets as Arnold saw them, to Wordsworth who could shrug off the weight of life to find and transmit in his verse the peace of nature,

> *He laid us as we lay at birth*
> *On the cool flowery lap of earth,*
> *Smiles broke from us and we had ease;*
> *The hills were round us, and the breeze*
> *Went o'er the sun-lit fields again.*

The scholar-gipsy has that kind of certitude which Arnold found in Wordsworth's poetry; the continued existence 'exempt from age' with which the poet endows him depends upon a continued averting of the eyes, an avoidance of life,

> *But fly our paths, our feverish contact fly!*
> *For strong the infection of our mental strife . . .*

The quality by which he earns his eternal youth is his devotion to '*one* aim, *one* business, *one* desire'; but this proves to be not so much an aim as a yearning for the vision to descend upon him, 'waiting for the spark from heaven to fall'. There is no prospect that this desire will ever be rewarded.

THE VANITY OF RHETORIC

The certitude lies in the fixed devotion to the hope, not in its fulfilment, and he will wander for ever,

> *Still nursing the unconquerable hope,*
> *Still clutching the inviolable shade.*

Arnold finds solace not in the completion of the journey of life, but in the image of the perpetually young gipsy for ever maintaining the freshness of his hope for a bright ending, for some revelation. The last two stanzas round the poem off with another of Arnold's sea images, this time of a Tyrian trader fleeing from the Greek invaders of his waters, as the scholar-gipsy is bidden to fly 'our greeting, fly our speech and smiles'. The trader turns westward, and voyages out into the unknown sea,

> *To where the Atlantic raves*
> *Outside the western straits; and unbent sails*
> *There, where down cloudy cliffs, through sheets of foam,*
> *Shy traffickers, the dark Iberians come;*
> *And on the beach undid his corded bales.*

The transference in these last last lines from the main image of the poem, the endless journey of the gipsy, to an image of another kind of journey, is a brilliant stroke, for the Tyrian trader does reach a goal in coming to land: thus the general image of wandering, travelling, finds completion in a journey's end, and the poem is given shape, but at the same time the scholar-gipsy is left to his wanderings.

The eternal quest of the scholar-gipsy, seeking but never finding, is a type of Arnold's own desire for a spark from heaven; what the poet lacks, yearns for, and creates in the figures, the gipsy, the Romantic poets, for whom he has a nostalgic regard, is the power of self-dedication. In *Thyrsis* he relates both Clough and himself to the scholar-gipsy,

> *A fugitive and gracious light he seeks,*
> *Shy to illumine; and I seek it too . . .*

> *Thou too, O Thyrsis, on like quest wast bound;*
> *Thou wanderedst with me for a little hour!*

MATTHEW ARNOLD'S POETRY

That light, the light of the unifying vision, is never attained; and unlike the scholar-gipsy, who is endowed with immortality,

> *Out of the heed of mortals he is gone,*
> *He wends unfollow'd, he must house alone;*
> *Yet on he fares, by his own heart inspired,*

Clough has died, and so must Arnold. Yet Clough always had 'visions of our light', believed that the quest might succeed, and virtue lies in maintaining that hope;

> *Why faintest thou? I wander'd till I died.*
> *Roam on! The light we sought is shining still.*

The ideal of self-dedication, represented in the scholar-gipsy's devotion to the quest, finds another image in the figure of the buried self in each of us; if we could but be true to this self, we might achieve a harmony with the universe, but we are distracted by the sick hurry and divided aims of life and fall into 'some bondage of the flesh or mind' from which we do not escape. So Empedocles speaks of life as a 'sad probation', sad because we fail the test,

> *To see if we will now at last be true*
> *To our own only true, deep buried selves,*
> *Being one with which we are one with the whole world.*

The image of the buried self is developed at length in *The Buried Life*, and is there linked with the image of the river of life in the idea of a buried stream beneath the surface on which we seem to be 'Eddying at large in blind uncertainty': it is our fate that

> *through the deep recesses of our breast*
> *The unregarded river of our life*
> *Pursue with indiscernible flow its way;*
> *And that we should not see*
> *The buried stream . . .*

THE VANITY OF RHETORIC

The yearning to track out 'our true, original course', to 'speak and act Our hidden self', is continually frustrated, and the sense of the buried life produces melancholy,

> *from time to time, vague and forlorn,*
> *From the soul's subterranean depth upborne*
> *As from an infinitely distant land,*
> *Come airs, and floating echoes, and convey*
> *A melancholy into all our day.*

There are moments when 'A man becomes aware of his life's flow', feels that his journey is bringing him to a goal, and when the 'heart lies plain', and the hidden self seems to be revealed. Such are the rare moments of love, as described in *The Buried Life*, 'When a beloved hand is laid in ours', and the moments, also rare, of faith that we are all

> *A single mood of the life*
> *Of the spirit in whom we exist,*
> *Who alone is all things in one.*

This kind of assertion reaches its climax in *Rugby Chapel*, in the image of the great dead, the 'pure souls' of the past, with whom Arnold's father is joined, giving courage to the rest of mankind to continue the journey of life,

> *On, to the bound of the waste,*
> *On, to the City of God.*

But belief seems usually nothing but 'a cry of desire' which is doomed to be unsatisfied, and the predominant note in Arnold's poetry is one of uncertainty, of disintegration, of failure to find a unifying vision and satisfy his wish

> *To have before my mind—instead*
> *Of the sick room, the mortal strife,*
> *The turmoil for a little breath—*
> *The pure eternal course of life . . .*

MATTHEW ARNOLD'S POETRY

His love poetry is poetry about separation; and his favourite image, that of the journey of life, receives a new orientation, because the desired goal, the achievement of the vision, seems impossible to attain, in the idea of a voyage continuing for ever, a quest never completed, and also in the idea of the true course of life being buried under the surface on which we aimlessly drift.

What affirmation there is in Arnold's poetry seems unimportant because it lacks the glow and thrill of the Romantic assertion; it provides a sad substitute for the vision of love in a 'struggling task'd morality', with its ideal of self-control, self-dependence, and release from passion. This is imaged in calm moonlight, the independent stillness of the stars, the calm motion of the sea: whatever token utterances he made occasionally to the contrary, his desire was not for involvement with the one life in and around us, but for withdrawal from that involvement in life which he felt to be necessary, and yet unavailing in his 'iron age'.

> *We, in some unknown Power's employ,*
> *Move on a rigorous line;*
> *Can neither when we will, enjoy,*
> *Nor, when we will, resign.*

'Fate drives me', he says, back from Obermann's world to his own course of life, where he is caught

> *Wandering between two worlds, one dead,*
> *The other powerless to be born,*
> *With nowhere yet to rest my head.*

The world of faith, of the vision of unity, of joy, is dead, and nothing has replaced it; all that remains is the desire to resign, to escape from the 'hot prison', the restlessness, the pain of life, into stillness like that of the stars or the sea, 'self-pois'd'.

It is not surprising then that his language proves often

THE VANITY OF RHETORIC

inadequate, especially in the rhetoric of assertion and the rhetoric of love. The vocabulary has become hollow, and is not supported by the imagery or the general tone of the poetry. Sometimes the effect is almost bathetic:

> *Sink, O youth, in thy soul!*
> *Yearn to the greatness of Nature;*
> *Rally the good in the depths of thyself!*

The image of the buried life in Arnold's poetry is effective as a type of the inaccessibility of the unifying vision, and conflicts here with the vocabulary of assertion: it is traditional to look upwards in aspiration, to seek good in the heights and evil in the depths. The idea of sinking in these lines is at odds with the idea of yearning to greatness, and their feebleness is due to this. Sometimes a clumsy vagueness of language and avoidance of the obvious and most compelling words, reduces the assertion to triviality:

> *Unquiet souls!*
> *—In the dark fermentation of earth,*
> *In the never idle workshop of nature,*
> *In the eternal movement,*
> *Ye shall find yourselves again!*

It is not pleasant to dwell on what happens to the dead in the 'workshop of nature', and this image conflicts with, rather than prepares for, the last two lines, which remain meaningless.

An inadequacy of language appears in many other passages of assertion. Often there is a kind of contradiction within the assertion, which seems to be withdrawn even as it is made. So for instance in *Obermann Once More*, the poet-recluse who speaks to Arnold in a vision ends his message on a note of optimism,

> *The world's great order dawns in sheen,*
> *After long darkness rude,*
> *Divinelier imaged, clearer seen,*
> *With happier zeal pursued.*

MATTHEW ARNOLD'S POETRY

He urges Arnold to use his powers to help men to attain joy, to 'tell Hope to a world new-made'; but between the statement that a new order has burst forth, and the exhortation, three stanzas intervene describing Arnold as joyless, powerless, old, 'dimm'd' and weak, and it seems hardly possible that this man should be the prophet of new hope, while

> *round thy firmer manhood cast,*
> *Hang weeds of our sad time.*

The word 'weeds' had been used in connexion with Obermann in *Stanzas from the Grande Chartreuse,*

> *The world, which for an idle day*
> *Grace to your mood of sadness gave,*
> *Long since hath flung her weeds away.*

Here the sense is clear, and the word can only refer to clothes; but in *Obermann Once More*, the meaning is confused, partly because the context limits it less precisely, partly because the word has already appeared in the poem in a quite different sense. The impact on the western world of Christianity is described by the visionary Obermann in terms of relief at the discovery of a solace for the spiritual desert of life; he says of 'the victorious West',

> *'Mid weeds and wrecks she stood—a place*
> *Of ruin—but she smiled!*

'Weeds of our sad time' seems to carry overtones of this, to suggest ruin, a wilderness, as well as clothes. Perhaps this is merely fanciful, but the contrast and implicit conflict between the new world dawning in brightness, 'clearer seen', and its prophet, sad, joyless, and 'dimm'd', is apparent.

Sometimes there is an uncertainty in the phrasing of the assertion, and the lack of conviction in the utterance reduces or destroys its force. One form this uncertainty takes is the use of a modifying 'haply', 'may', or some such means of

THE VANITY OF RHETORIC

withdrawing from a commitment to a belief; so *The Future* ends with the hope that

> *Haply the river of Time . . .*
> *May acquire, if not the calm*
> *Of its early mountainous shore,*
> *Yet a solemn peace of its own;*

and *The Buried Life*, after describing the rare moments when 'a lost pulse of feeling stirs again', and the poet finds release from the burden of life in the revelation of a nobler, inward life, moments when 'the heart lies plain', ends by implying that the revelation may be an illusion after all, as the word 'thinks' cancels the certainty:

> *And then he thinks he knows*
> *The hills where his life rose,*
> *And the sea where it goes.*

Another form of uncertainty appears in *A Wish*, in which the poet asks that on his deathbed he may become one with the universe and feel 'The pure eternal course of life'; but this ennobling vision of becoming 'wed' in soul to the everlasting

> *world which was ere I was born,*
> *The world which lasts when I am dead,*

is suddenly dropped at the end of the poem, where, instead of the glow of a release into a new unity, the transfiguration which might be expected as a climax, there is simply resignation to the doubt of 'To work *or* wait elsewhere *or* here':

> *Thus feeling, gazing, might I grow*
> *Compos'd, refresh'd ennobled, clear;*
> *Then willing let my spirit go*
> *To work or wait elsewhere or here!*

Perhaps a less obvious way in which an assertion is weakened is in a confusion or vagueness of ideas or in a syntactical obscurity. An instance may be found in *Rugby Chapel*,

> *See! In the rocks of the world*
> *Marches the host of mankind,*
> *A feeble wavering line.*
> *Where are they tending?—A God*
> *Marshall'd them, gave them their goal.*

In this image as it relates to its context there is a double ambiguity. It is part of the image of the journey of life on which the whole poem is based; the course of most men has been described as 'an eddy of purposeless dust', and the few who, like the poet, seek to advance to 'a clear-purposed goal' are set off from the crowd, in their lonely, difficult journeying. Yet now, towards the end of the poem, the 'host of mankind' suddenly appears to be engaged on the same journey as the few, a transference perhaps reflected in the contrast between the images of a marching host and a 'feeble wavering line'. The host, whose lives had been described as 'without aim', are now also suddenly given an aim, not one of their own choosing, but one prescribed by 'A God'; great souls like the poet's father have been called a few lines earlier, 'Servants of God', and the question arises, are these the same God? It would seem not, for the great souls are dedicated to the Christian God, whereas the other God represents merely a kind of fate, pushing men through life. This passage illustrates the rhetorical jugglery in which Arnold became involved when he sought to crown a poem expressing a melancholy view of life in his time with an ending of assertion which is not fully supported by the main theme; the cry

> *On, to the bounds of the waste,*
> *On, to the City of God,*

rings a little hollow after the terrible picture drawn in the first 130 lines of the poem. In the same way, the note of optimism at the end of *A Summer Night*,

THE VANITY OF RHETORIC
How fair a lot to fill
Is left to each man still!

is not really supported by the main body of the poem; this describes two ways of life, that of the majority, a meaningless, prison-like existence, and that of 'the rest', who seek contact with the eternal, but disappear in the search for a 'false, impossible shore'; these two ways account for all men, and the transference to an assertive ending is achieved only by means of an apostrophe to the heavens, which are doubtfully and vaguely drawn into an association with man's life, for they

though so noble, share in the world's toil,
And, though so task'd keep free from dust and soil!
I will not say that your mild deeps retain
A tinge, it may be, of their silent pain
Who have long'd deeply once, and long'd in vain—
But I will rather say that you remain
A world above man's head, to let him see
How boundless might his soul's horizons be . . .

The heavens thus become an example for man, and seem to offer a third way of life ('How good it were to abide there . . .'); but it is not clear how they 'share in the world's toil', and the assertion that they are involved in human suffering is characteristically withdrawn even as it is made, in the phrase 'I will *not* say that . . .'.

An inadequacy of language is also seen in the intrusion on a number of occasions of a *deus ex machina* in the person of Fate, or of a god which is the equivalent of fate. This offered the poet a tactic for evading issues raised in his poems, and helped him sometimes to slip into an assertive ending not fully justified by the rest of the poem, as noted above in the case of *Rugby Chapel*, at other times to avoid making the assertion demanded by the rest of the poem. The most prominent example of this is in the Marguerite poems; in *Meeting* the poet is about to leap ashore to welcome her, his 'bliss', but instead of the expected culmination, there is a

MATTHEW ARNOLD'S POETRY

sudden transposition to a language that would have been appropriate in some early eighteenth-century poetry; accents which might have sounded well in *The Rape of the Lock* seem strangely out of key here:

> *I know that graceful figure fair,*
> *That cheek of languid hue;*
> *I know that soft, enkerchief'd hair,*
> *And those sweet eyes of blue.*
>
> *Again I spring to make my choice;*
> *Again in tones of ire*
> *I hear a God's tremendous voice:*
> *'Be counsell'd, and retire'.*

This failure of language in the rhetoric of assertion and the rhetoric of love reflects the most terrible feature of Arnold's poetry, the disintegration of the Romantic vision. A struggling task'd morality is substituted for the vision of love, an image of absolute peace in isolation; and the vision of the one life within us and abroad is replaced by the ideal of the self-dependent single life, calm and free from passion.

II

Arnold's poetry marks the disintegration of the Romantic vision of unity into 'Poor fragments of a broken world'. The decay of the vision coincided with the rise of the modern urban, industrialized society. In Wordsworth's *Prelude* the city is a symbol of the spiritual desert, the 'wide waste' through which the poet passes to find restoration and renewed faith in the permanent forms of nature. But there is no escape from the city for Arnold, except in temporary excursions into a nostalgically regarded past, into the wish-fulfilment of *The Scholar Gipsy*, or into unsubstantial assertions of hope or faith. He knew that the old world was dead, its faith gone, and his finest poetry expresses his sense of isolation in life, not of unity—it is the theme, for instance, of

THE VANITY OF RHETORIC

Sohrab and Rustum as well as of many of the more personal poems—his sense of

> *Wandering between two worlds, one dead,*
> *The other powerless to be born.*

In particular, the city provided a basis for images of the 'strange disease of modern life', life as a struggle on a 'darkling plain', where the millions suffer and grieve, and

> *most men in a brazen prison live,*
> *Where, in the sun's hot eye,*
> *With heads bent o'er their toil, they languidly*
> *Their lives to some unmeaning taskwork give . . .*

The decay of the Romantic vision also coincided with the growth of a new audience for poetry. The decline of the aristocratic world of the eighteenth century with its hierarchy of ordered values had sent the Romantic poets scurrying into their own souls in search of a new scale of values and a new mode of communication to replace the formal poetic diction of their predecessors. Each created his own order, in terms usually of the vision of love or the journey of life, and each was able to oppose to the flux of a world of broken values, to the anarchy of individualism, symbols of that order in the beauty and permanence of the natural world. The first half of the nineteenth century brought enormous changes to the land, in an astonishing increase of population, of industry and urban growth, and an influx of people into the cities. Perhaps the principal agent in this was the railway, which brought a revolution in communications, stimulated the growth of the coal and steel industries, and soon left no part of the country remoter than a few hours by train from the cities. The Stockton and Darlington railway was opened in 1825, long after the best work of Coleridge and Wordsworth was done, and soon after the deaths of Keats (1821), Shelley (1822), and Byron (1824); and by 1850 the country was covered with a network of lines. This rapid growth created a new aristocracy of the moneyed man, the prosperous businessman and industrialist, who achieved success through luck and ruthlessness often, and whose world depended on what seemed to be the independent laws of the market, of supply and demand. It was, and remains, a world of anarchical values, ruled by mysterious economic laws which seem to operate of their own accord. Although this community was stable during England's prosperity, its individual members might change—society is never more fluid than when a man may make a fortune and just as soon lose a fortune—and drop back into the bottomless pit of the poor through some accident of the market.[1] Perhaps because of this lack of security, and the lack of a tradition in a new-made society whose members lived a relatively precarious existence, they sought in poetry and art an unchanging, stable world, unlike their own, and a celebration of tradition and traditional things, a respect for the outward signs of an older order, for titles, royalty, and the church.

Their art is represented in the poetry of the laureate Tennyson, in *The Idylls of the King*, with their courtliness, their absurdly high moral tone, and their evocation of a vanished age; and in the dream-world of romance created, for instance, in Morris's *The Earthly Paradise*, with its apology,

> *The heavy trouble, the bewildering care*
> *That weighs us down who live and earn our bread,*
> *These idle verses have no power to bear;*
> *So let me sing of names remembered,*
> *Because they, living not, can ne'er be dead,*
> *Or long time take their memory quite away*
> *From us poor singers of an empty day.*[2]

[1] The popular novels of Dickens reflect this kind of society; whereas in Jane Austen's novels wealth, a competence at any rate, had been assumed, and the real rewards for the heroines are measured in terms of honour and a good marriage, the novels of Dickens frequently portray a hero's rise from poverty to wealth, and money often seems the ultimate reward.

[2] Morris was of course aware that he lived in an 'empty day', but the huge romance comments no further on it.

THE VANITY OF RHETORIC

Their art is represented also in the optimism of Browning's later poetry, in the patriotic thunder of Tennyson and later of Kipling; and again, it is represented in the easy piety of Mrs Browning's verse and much other poetry of the time. These were some of the qualities they looked for, and if they found any of them, they could ignore other aspects of a work and interpret it to fit their pattern. The most interesting example of this was the reception of *In Memoriam*, in which a 'vast majority' of critics 'found the theology sound and the faith inspiring',[1] and for long it served as a poem of religious consolation and uplift.[2] The late Victorian popularity of Tennyson and Browning, both of whom matured well before Victoria ascended the throne, was based upon an interpretation of their central achievement in accordance with the demand for piety, optimism, and a high moral tone; and the rhetoric of the vision of love, which they retained after the vision had begun to disintegrate, and which emerges in empty assertions, lent colour to such an interpretation.[3]

The most exciting poets of this period are those who rebelled against such values, like Swinburne with his pagan sensuality and disrespect for Browning and Tennyson, to whose verse 'soothed Britannia simpers in serene applause'[4]; and above all those who recognized the real poverty of spirit, the isolation of the individual, the lack of security and of an ordered scale of values in the new urban society. The city, 'the great town's harsh, heart-wearying roar', was at once the symptom and symbol of the ugliness and loneliness behind the façade of optimism for a few poets like Arnold, and William Morris in his socialist poems, who asked

> *How long shall they reproach us where crowd on crowd they dwell,*
> *Poor ghosts of the wicked city, the gold-crushed hungry hell?*

---

[1] Edgar Finley Shannon, *Tennyson and the Reviewers*, p. 149.

[2] Bradley in his *Commentary* (1901) speaks still of the ordinary reader's delight in its teaching, its 'consoling or uplifting thoughts' (pp. 36-37).

[3] See above, p. 135.

[4] Cited from a manuscript poem of Swinburne's in C. K. Hyder, *Swinburne's Literary Career and Fame* (Duke University Press, 1933), p. 19.

THOMSON'S *THE CITY OF DREADFUL NIGHT*

The most remarkable sequel to Arnold's poetry in the later nineteenth century, a poem which marks the complete disintegration of the Romantic vision, was James Thomson's *The City of Dreadful Night*. This inverts the rhetoric and the images of the Romantic vision, and applies them to an assertion of despair, the negation of that vision. It was a reflection of the character of the fashionable audience for poetry that one critic began his review of the poem by saying, 'We start from the basis that pessimism is heresy'.[1]

It is an uneven poem, but one of great power because the rhetoric, though crude, is sustained by the themes and imagery. The poem arose primarily out of Thomson's own frustrations, his poverty, loneliness and bad health, and reflects his bitterness and his rejection of Christianity. But at the same time, the city of the poem represents London, and is a type of all cities; frustration, rootlessness and insecurity are common to many of the lonely crowd[2] which inhabits modern towns. The image Thomson created was a terrifying one; instead of the noise, bustle and throng which are the most obvious and superficial characteristics of city-life, he depicted 'soundless solitudes immense' as of a sleeping city, where those inhabitants who wander in the streets rarely speak to one another, and where, though the street-lamps burn, the houses are nearly all 'still as tombs' and dark. Although the image begins from the lonely city of 3 a.m., of silent streets and empty squares, it is modified in two ways. Firstly, it has many associations with hell or limbo; the only hope for its inhabitants is death, yet a night 'seems termless hell'; their existence is a 'Death-in-Life', recalling the spectre-like figure of Coleridge's *Ancient Mariner*, and 'Death-in-Life is the eternal king' of that region, where they wander,

---

[1] In the *London Quarterly Review*, April 1881, cited in Imogene B. Walker, *James Thomson (B.V.). A Critical Study*, (Ithaca, New York, 1950), p. 136n.

[2] The phrase is borrowed from the title of the book by David Riesman, in collaboration with Reuel Denney and Nathan Glazer (New Haven, Conn., 1950), a study of the 'middleclass urban American of today' who 'remains a lonely member of the crowd because he never comes really close to the others or to himself' (Preface, p. v).

THE VANITY OF RHETORIC

like the mariner, under the burden of their doom; like him, too, some of these figures, half-phantoms, half-men,

> *I have seen phantoms there that were as men*
> *And men that were as phantoms flit and roam,*
> (414-15)

seem constrained to tell 'of ancient woes and black defeats'. As the poem proceeds, the city is given a religious 'location' as a limbo, whose inhabitants are shut out 'alike from Heaven and Earth and Hell', and this is related to the psychological 'location' of the opening. For the city is set between a wilderness and a sea, so that the entire landscape is made up of what had been for Wordsworth symbols of the waste of suffering which men must endure; only now the wilderness includes among its features many of the natural objects, like valleys and mountains, which had been sources of strength and consolation for him and other Romantic poets.

> *A trackless wilderness rolls north and west,*
> *Savannahs, savage woods, enormous mountains,*
> *Bleak uplands, black ravines with torrent fountains;*
> *And eastward rolls the shipless sea's unrest:*
> (74-77)

Whereas for Wordsworth restoration had followed suffering, in an escape from the city and desert to the vision of unity on Snowdon, and the ancient mariner comes back home after his terrible journey, the city in this poem is the end of the journey, and once there,

> *Escape seems hopeless to the heart forlorn.* (317)

It can only be reached by a journey of suffering,

> *Athwart the mountains and immense wild tracts,*
> *Or flung a waif upon that vast sea-flow,*
> *Or down the river's boiling cataracts:*
> *To reach it is as dying fever-stricken.* (310-13)

THOMSON'S *THE CITY OF DREADFUL NIGHT*

One such journey is described in detail in Section IV, through a desert where a landscape of horror heaves and burns with continual threat to the lone figure striding through[1] without hope; and when hope comes to him, it comes in the form of beauty mixed with anguish and desolation, of love already involved with death, in the figure of the woman carrying her bleeding heart in her hand. The woman, symbol of the love that might have saved him from despair, is dead even as she reaches him in her 'snow-white shroud', and this kills his better self, symbolized in the 'corpse-like' figure which the sea carries away in her embrace, the sea which is here a figure for the oblivion of death. His other self of those 'Two selves distinct that cannot join again' is left forlorn, hope and love gone again, and only rage and fear remaining, to reach the city.[2] The journey brings him, as a similar journey has brought the other inhabitants, to the city from which the only escape is death, the city which is limbo, a wilderness at the heart of the wilderness.

In this way the image of the city of 3 a.m. is generalized into a symbol of a spiritual wilderness. A second way in which the image is modified is by its relation, in a special and grotesque manner, to the familiar life of the daylight city, which contrasts with the terrible imaginary landscape of its unfamiliar setting. Although the city seems silent and empty, the eye there learns a new vision and the ear a new hearing, discerning shadows moving in the gloom and murmurs of voices,

> *The ear, too, with the silence vast and deep*
> *Becomes familiar though not reconciled;*
> *Hears breathings as of hidden life asleep,*
> *And muffled throbs as of pent passions wild,*
> *Far murmurs, speech of pity or derision . . .*   (189-93)

[1] It may be compared with the landscape of Browning's *Childe Roland to the Dark Tower Came*, where, in contrast, Roland's quest ends in a dazzle of light and reunion with his companions in death.

[2] The autobiographical background of this section is irrelevant to this discussion; the negation of love in death, contrasting with the Romantic triumph of love in death (*The Eve of St. Agnes*), is another of those reversals of the Romantic position in the poem, cf. Section X, and p. 175 below.

THE VANITY OF RHETORIC

A strange parody of daily life goes on under the 'reign of terror', the 'lawless law' of the king, Death-in-Life; figures walk the streets and squares aimlessly, a speaker stands addressing an empty square 'As if large multitudes were gathered round', and a shadowy congregation listens to a sermon in the vast cathedral. The various anonymous characters who figure in the poem are spoken of as men and women, and are part of the population of a city where, as in life,

> *some are great in rank and wealth and power,*
> *And some renowned for genius and for worth;*
> *And some are poor and mean, who brood and cower*
> *And shrink from notice, and accept all dearth*
> *Of body, heart and soul, and leave to others*
> *All boons of life . . .* (579-84)

The dwellers of the city are at once phantom-like and human; the rich and the poor mingle in streets and by an elm-lined river and near the great cathedral, which are just sufficient to hint at London, but if in one sense they seem substantial enough, in another, they are 'the flitting shadows of a dream'. The most striking episode in the building up of this relationship of the city to life is Section XII, in which various figures are described entering the cathedral, each giving a countersign to a hooded personage at the door; their words make a parody of a litany, with the refrain 'I wake from daydreams to this real night'. The 'daydreams' are various modes of living, those of the poet, ruler, painter, warrior, and the like, so that by this device dream and reality are transposed, and the city becomes more real than real life.

The two aspects of the city, as a terrible and fantastic imaginary world, a limbo of the lost, set in a symbolic landscape and peopled with unreal symbolic figures, and as a real city with its elm-lined river, its streets and squares, its human life, are confused and mingled in the poem. The city is at once a place of solitude, and a place teeming with its strange life, for 'Although not many exiles wander there', the 'I' of the poem constantly meets them, men walking alone, or companions on the river-bank, the congregation in the cathedral, the suicides who plunge into the river night by night; it is at once 'soundless' and still, and full of noise, the voices of the many speakers in the poem, throbs of lamentation, the 'trampling crash of heavy ironshod feet' as a huge wagon rolls by, the crashing fall of the statues in Section XX; it is a place at once of death and of life, of 'Death-in-Life'; its inhabitants seem to be both phantoms and men at the same time; 'They are most rational and yet insane'; and the city of night as a whole is both real, a place reached by men who, in an image reminiscent of Shelley's poetry, 'pierce life's pleasant veil of various error', and unreal, dissolving in daylight 'like a dream of night away'. The remote and the familiar, the imaginary and the actual are united, so that none can

> Discern that dream from real life in aught.
> For life is but a dream whose shapes return . . .
> (56-57)

The city then, in its dual character representing both a very real condition of men in urban society, the isolation of the individual in the crowd, and a symbol, inherited from the Romantic poets, of a spiritual desert, is the most appropriate vehicle for a rejection of the Romantic assertion. The action of the poem employs the images of the journey of life and the vision of love, two of the major Romantic images, but the context of the city is new, the goal of the journey and the climax of the vision different; instead of unity in 'the one life', there is loneliness and separation. The description of a journey to the city in Section IV has been discussed; the culmination of the traveller's progress through the desert is his arrival in the city, which is another type of the desert, and from which there is no escape. To arrive is not to cease from wandering, but rather to be doomed to roam without ceasing, and with no prospect of a further goal except death and oblivion. This is imaged in several figures, particularly in

THE VANITY OF RHETORIC

Sections II and XVIII. In the first of these sections the 'I' of the poem follows one wanderer as he travels 'weary roads without suspense' on a pilgrimage to the 'shrines'[1] where faith, hope and love died; the purpose he seemed to have proves to be no purpose at all, but simply an aimless repetition of the same walks, while

> *He circled thus for ever tracing out*
> *The series of the fraction left of Life;*
> *Perpetual recurrence in the scope*
> *Of but three terms, dead Faith, dead Love, dead Hope.*
> (171-4)

If it leads anywhere, the journey brings the traveller not to an achievement of faith, but to the death of faith. Even hell provides no resting-place for such men who have no hope, and so cannot pay the 'settled toll' for entry by casting away hope; Section VI offers another example of this type of wanderer, in the two companions engaged on a hopeless search throughout 'this Limbo's dreary scope' for 'some minute lost hope'. The most terrifying inversion of the image of the journey of life comes in Section XVIII, where the speaker approaches a deformed, bestial creature crawling painfully along, the degenerate figure of what 'had been a man'; the creature alternately threatens and pleads with him as if he has come to steal a secret, the clue that he imagines will lead him back

> *From this accursed night without a morn,*
> *And through the deserts which have else no track,*
> *And through vast wastes of horror-haunted time,*
> *To Eden innocence in Eden's clime.* (935-8)

The final despairing hope of the wanderer is not for a goal to the journey, but that he may cancel it altogether, retrace his life to 'antenatal night',

[1] This recalls the strong element of a pilgrimage in *The Prelude*; see above, p. 64.

> *And hide his elements in that large womb.* (949)

All such attempts of the city's inhabitants to escape or to find a goal are futile, for they are doomed to remain 'spectral wanderers of unholy night' until death, complete oblivion, comes to them. Living, they have only the choice of desert or desert, and the one way out is suicide, to leap into the river, or to glide out in a boat,

> *drifting down into the desert ocean*
> *To starve or sink from out the desert world.* (969-70)

As the journey of life now leads nowhere, so the vision of love is distorted, and instead of culminating in a triumphant unity in death, a dying into life, it ends in separation, loneliness and despair through the premature death of one partner. This is the image presented in Section IV, in which the woman, the love, that might have brought hope to the voyager through the desert, and might have rescued him from it, proves to be dead as they meet; and there is a ghastly parody of the Romantic vision of unity in the union of two corpse-like figures floating out on that ocean which only seems to be an extension of the desert. Their 'doom is drear', and it is a union of death not life, an incomplete one at that, for it leaves the viler self, of those two selves 'distinct that cannot join again' into which the voyager is divided, to continue his terrible aimless journey to the city. The theme is taken up again in Section X, where, in an inversion of another common Romantic image, that of light representing the achievement of love, the one mansion in all the city that is flooded with light is a house of death and separation. For in it a beautiful woman,

> *A woman very young and very fair:*
> *Beloved by bounteous life and joy and youth,*
> *And loving these sweet lovers, so that care*
> *And age and death seemed not for her in sooth . . .,*
>   (513-16)

lies dead, while her lover mourns, conscious that she will 'never wake'. He thinks of the possibilities of living on to grieve over her death and mourn his separation from her, or of dying and so ending his grief, but at the same time losing sight of his 'dear vision' altogether; and renounces 'all choice of life and death', desiring only to remain at her side for ever. They are left thus, together, but eternally separated.

The death of faith, love and hope is imaged in these inversions of the Romantic vision, which *The City of Dreadful Night* negates. The poem negates also the Christian assertion into which the Victorian poets, Tennyson, Browning and the later Wordsworth had deviated as a modification of or a substitute for the Romantic vision. This theme runs through the central sections of the poem; the inhabitants of the city, shut out from heaven, rail against the wickedness of the God who created the misery of the world,

> *the ignominious guilt*
> *Of having made such men in such a world.*
>
> (451-2)

But comfort comes to them in the sermon delivered to them in the cathedral, bringing, in its parody of a Christmas hymn,

> *Good tidings of great joy for you, for all;*
> *There is no God . . .* (724-5)

One man in the congregation protests that life is a cheat, that there is no comfort for him since the pleasures of living have proved to be a delusion; and the pulpit speaker replies that this is what they must recognize, that there is nothing good in life, and their only comfort then lies in the oblivion before and after:

> *My Brother, my poor Brother, it is thus;*
> *This life itself holds nothing good for us,*
> *But it ends soon and nevermore can be:*
> *And we knew nothing of it ere our birth,*
> *And shall know nothing when consigned to earth:*
> *I ponder these thoughts and they comfort me.*
>
> (845-50)

THOMSON'S *THE CITY OF DREADFUL NIGHT*

The religious vision is thus also inverted, and instead of comfort being found in the prospect of heaven, the only consolation for the city's people rests in the certainty that life ends absolutely with death. Even that last refuge of the vision in Matthew Arnold's poetry, the 'pure dark regions' of the heavens which, as in *A Summer Night*, seem to point the way to a better life for man, to show him 'How boundless might his soul's horizons be', is rejected:

> *men regard with passionate awe and yearning*
> *The mighty marching and the golden burning,*
> *And think the heavens respond to what they feel,*
> (855-7)

but they are fools to do so, for 'There is no heart or mind in all their splendour'; the heavens are merely a 'void abyss', the stars worlds as dreary as our own, and as subject to change, and it is idle to look there for images of eternity, for

> *The spheres eternal are a grand illusion.* (877)

The City of Dreadful Night is built out of these inversions or distortions of images which had been fundamental to the Romantic vision. After the opening sections which present images of the city as desert, and of the city's inhabitants in their aimless wandering, there is an alternation of short and long sections. The short ones are descriptive, amplifying the picture of the city and its people, and contributing to that strange atmosphere of confusion between dream and reality, where the silence is full of sound (Section III), where the men are dead and yet 'as if new-born' (Section V), where the living look like phantoms and phantoms look like the living (Section VII), where all are 'most rational and yet insane' (Section XI), and suffer doubly, yearning for death to end the 'nights that are as aeons of slow pain' (Section XIII), but clutching illusions which prevent them from seeking death. The longer sections present the images discussed above, of the journey and of love (Sections IV, VI, X, and

THE VANITY OF RHETORIC

XVIII in particular), and of religion (Sections VIII, XIV, XVI). Finally, as the poem begins so it ends, with two sections of a more general character. The first, Section XX, contains a last, general image of the death of faith, love and hope, which the wanderer of Section II had bewailed, in the statues of the angel and the warrior, representing the noblest aspirations of man, which fall shattered before the feet of the sphinx, the symbol of necessity, with its

> *cold majestic face,*
> *Whose vision seemed of infinite void space.*
> (1038-9)

Section XXI returns to the city as a whole, and then creates an image of its presiding 'Patroness and Queen', based on Dürer's picture of Melencolia, a 'titanic' statue overlooking the city, and forming at once a model for the inhabitants, and a summation of all their characteristics. This is the final inversion, the substitute for the Romantic aspiration in this goddess-like figure to which the city's people look for strength 'And confirmation of the old despair'. Instead of hope and joy, she gives them the certainties which alone make life bearable, and which are the reverse of the Romantic assertions,

> *The sense that every struggle brings defeat*
>   *Because Fate holds no prize to crown success;*
> *That all the oracles are dumb or cheat*
>   *Because they have no secret to express;*
> *That none can pierce the vast black veil uncertain*
>   *Because there is no light beyond the curtain;*
> *That all is vanity and nothingness.* (1103-9)

For the Romantic poets the city had been a type of the spiritual wilderness from which escape was possible, but for Thomson it has become the true centre of life from which there is no escape. Although Thomson's vision, with its absolute negation is a limited and partial one, it is more true and valuable than that of the other poets of his time. The city

THOMSON'S *THE CITY OF DREADFUL NIGHT*

had become the centre of life, and the poetry of the future was bound sooner or later to recognize this and seek to come to terms with it. But it was a long process; for many years the dominant poets catered for an audience which did not want to see the chaos in its midst, and perhaps in a period of expansion, prosperity and world-domination, did not need to see it. Poems of romance, using the rhetoric of the Romantic poets without their sustaining imagery or overriding vision; poems of natural description, employing the diction and sometimes the imagery of the Romantic poets, without their visionary splendour and rhetoric; and poems of patriotic fervour or of an easy religious consolation were written in large numbers. The best of them, *The Earthly Paradise*, the lyrics of Coventry Patmore and Christina Rossetti, Tennyson's *The Revenge*, are good in their kind, but have only a narrow or marginal reference to life as a whole. The reaction towards art for art's sake at the end of the nineteenth century was a movement in the wrong direction, seeking an escape from science and materialism in the absolute beauty and what was claimed to be spirituality of the perfection of form; it was an esoteric movement, based upon the attitude that 'the whole mystery of beauty can never be comprehended by the crowd'.[1] At the same time, it brought the first attack on the use of empty rhetoric in poetry, of words as counters to produce a stock response, and of debased Romantic modes of writing, and encouraged in their stead a more precise use of words, a habit of allusion and irony, and an avoidance of the vague. This was the first step towards a new diction, and pointed to later developments, helping to make possible a fresh exploration of the human situation by modern poets like Yeats, T. S. Eliot and W. H. Auden, and a new attempt to make order out of the chaos that is still with us. It is significant that one of the most influential modern poems has been *The Waste Land*, a poem of the city.

[1] Arthur Symons, *The Symbolist Movement in Literature*, p. 36.

CONCLUSION

It is no longer possible for the modern poet to turn his face from the city as the Romantics could; the city is a great fact of modern life. During the nineteenth century the Romantic assertion gradually diminished in scope, until it was negated in *The City of Dreadful Night*. The vocabulary of assertion became detached from those images of impression which had supported it, and decayed into empty rhetoric; and the images ceased to be appropriate, as the natural world became less important and less accessible to the majority of people. Detached from the assertion, images drawn from the natural world tended to become what on the whole they have remained, vehicles of a sentimental appeal. But in seeking to come to terms with the city, the modern poet has to account for a world in which the lonely crowd is lonelier even than for the Romantics, in which the isolation of the individual is more marked, in which the city dominates everything and everyone. The problem these poets faced, of taming chaos into order, remains, but the modern poet reflects, in his reluctance to commit himself to any kind of assertion, a common loss of faith in an ultimate solution. If he does commit himself, it is to that old man's rage for life of Yeats, or to a withdrawal into an authoritarian religion, such as T. S. Eliot made.[1]

The prevailing contemporary poetry is poetry of conflict, which makes no assertion, refuses to commit itself, is witty, ironic, or content with a neutral tone, and it may generally be said to reflect the contradictory elements of experience not because the business of poetry is to reflect discordant im-

---
[1] Those modern poets like Dylan Thomas who have made a vigorous assertion, do not reflect the dominant tone of the present time.

CONCLUSION

pulses, but because no resolution seems satisfactory for our time. This poetry of conflict has brought release from the bondage of rhetoric into which late nineteenth-century poetry tended to fall, but it has its limitations. It is poetry for a small public, and is intellectual, often esoteric; much of it descants upon 'the supreme theme of art and song', is poetry about poetry, like that of Wallace Stevens, or a number of poems in the recent anthology *New Lines*,[1] or it is poetry in which the structure, the wit, counts for all, and the poet's experience seems empty; as one critic has said,

> if the structures of expression are to be more interesting to the reader than the structures of experience behind them, the only way to induce the right sort of attention in the reader is to have nothing behind them at all, that is, to have poems that are meaningless. The only alternative is to have poems that talk about themselves. . . .[2]

This poetry has brought in its train a body of criticism devoted to explaining and defending it, and which sets a supreme value upon poetry of conflict in general, upon metaphor as opposed to the image of impression, and upon irony as opposed to the vocabulary of assertion. In setting up the new gods much energy has been given to knocking down the old ones and discarding them. But perhaps the time will come when their assertion will seem more valuable than the response of our poets of conflict: meanwhile it is losing sight of their achievement to attack them for making an assertion. We might more appropriately envy them their ability to do so, and take comfort from their courageous affirmation of a vision of harmony, and of the possible greatness of man.

[1] Edited by Robert Conquest, 1956.
[2] Donald Davie, *Articulate Energy. An Inquiry into the Syntax of English Poetry* (1955), p. 93.

INDEX

Abrams, M. H. 17n., 121n.
Anderson, Ruth L., 40
Aristotle, 26, 27
Arnold, Matthew, 150-66, 168-9, 177
Auden, W. H., 47n., 53n., 135n., 179
Austen, Jane, 167n.

Baker, Carlos, 98n., 99n.
Ballad, The, 24, 51
Barfield, Owen, 18n.
Bayley, John, 11n.
Bible, The, 54
Bion, 98n.
Blake, William, 36
Bodkin, Maud, 24, 53n.
Bradley, A. C., 122n., 135n., 168n.
Brandenburg, Alice S., 25n., 31n.
Brooks, Cleanth, 19n., 20n., 21n., 22n.
Brown, S. J., 26
Browning, Elizabeth Barrett, 168
Browning, Robert, 138-48, 149, 150, 168, 171n., 176
  Men and Women, 116, 138-48, 149-50
  Ring and the Book, The, 139n.
  Sordello, 139
Bunyan, John, 64n.
Byron, George Gordon, Lord, 57, 101, 166
  Don Juan, 42, 56, 57

Carlyle, Thomas, 17, 120
Chapman, George, 98n.
Chatterton, Thomas, 102
City, The, as a poetic image, 44, 47-8, 49, 65-6, 68-70, 165-6, 169-79, 181
Clough, Arthur Hugh, 156
Coleridge, Samuel Taylor, 22, 46-7, 56, 64, 65, 80, 166
  Biographia Literaria, 42-3, 55
  Destiny of Nations, The, 47
  Religious Musings, 41, 47
  Rime of the Ancient Mariner, The, 26, 30, 45, 46, 51, 53-5, 58, 60, 64, 68, 81, 111, 169, 170
  Statesman's Manual, The, 45
Conquest, Robert, 182n.

Davie, Donald, 182
Davies, Sir John, 40
De la Primaudaye, Pierre, 41
Denney, Reuel, 169n.
De Selincourt, Ernest, 59n., 67n.
Desert, The, as a poetic image, 47-8, 49, 53, 54, 68, 69, 72, 73, 165, 170-6
Dickens, Charles, 167n.
Donne, John, 25, 30, 32, 37

Eliot, T. S., 12-14, 16, 18, 20, 24, 135n., 179, 181
  Love Song of J. Alfred Prufrock, The, 30, 32
  Waste Land, The, 16, 37, 179

183

INDEX

Gibbs, J. W. M., 17n.
Glanvil, Joseph, 155
Glazer, Nathan, 169n.
Graves, Robert, 21n.

Hallam, A. H., 47, 153
   and *In Memoriam*, 121-38
   review of Tennyson's *Poems, Chiefly Lyrical*, 116-17
Havens, R. D., 67n.
Herrick, Robert, 36
House, Humphry, 135n.
Hulme, T. E., 11-12, 14, 18, 20
Hungerford, E. B., 98n.
Hunt, J. H. Leigh, 101
Hyder, C. K., 168n.

Imagery (*see also* City, Desert, Journey, Light, Love, Sea, Vocabulary of Assertion), 17-38
Images of Impression, 31-2, 34-8, 45-50, 55, 69-70, 74-5, 79, 80-1, 93, 103-10, 112-15, 123-34, 150-60, 173-8, 181
Images of Thought, 31-4, 35-8
Metaphor, 16-30
Simile, 23, 29

Jones, Robert, 67n.
Journey, The, as a poetic image, 50, 51-5, 60-9, 91n., 131, 149-59, 173-5

Keats, John, 46, 80-94, 97, 100, 107, 108, 110, 116, 117, 121, 166
   Endymion, 46, 82-5, 93, 95

Keats, John (*cont.*)
   Eve of St. Agnes, The, 81, 85-94, 95, 107, 108, 110, 111, 112, 171n.
   Hyperion, 46, 56-7, 58, 94
   La Belle Dame sans Merci, 51-5, 58, 60
   Letters, 57
Kermode, Frank, 11, 14, 16
Kipling, Rudyard, 168

Langbaum, Robert, 138-9n.
Language, *see* Imagery; Vocabulary of Assertion
Leavis, F. R., 20n., 22n., 31
Lewis, Cecil Day, 25
Lewis, C. S., 31n.
Light, as a poetic image, 46-7, 69, 74, 105-7, 112-14, 124-30, 156-7, 175-6
Love, as a poetic image, 50, 80-110, 111, 116, 118, 123, 129, 133-4, 138-9, 143-8, 149-50, 158-9, 164-5, 173, 175-6
Lucan, 102
Lyell, Charles, 135n.

Mallarmé, Etienne (Stéphane), 21
Mattes, Eleanor B., 135n.
Metaphor, *see* Imagery
Mill, John Stuart, 17n.
Milton, John, 100
   Lycidas, 98n., 99n.
   Paradise Lost, 34-5, 37, 57, 59, 99n.
Moore, Thomas, 101
Morris, William, 167, 168, 179
Moschus, 98n.

INDEX

Murry, J. Middleton, 18, 26

New Lines, 182

Patmore, Coventry, 179
Poe, Edgar Allan, 25
Poetic Imagery, see Imagery
Poetry of Conflict, 37-8, 139n., 181-2
Pope, Alexander, 43-5, 165
Pottle, F. A., 22n., 31n.
Potts, Abbie Findlay, 59n., 64n.
Pound, Ezra, 11
'Power', as a value-word in The Prelude, 76-9

Ransom, John Crowe, 24
Rhetoric (see also Vocabulary of Assertion), 24-5, 112, 117, 137, 159-65, 178-9
Richards, I. A., 18-19
Riding, Laura, 21n.
Riesman, David, 169n.
Rossetti, Christina, 179

Sea, The, as a poetic image, 37, 54, 61, 68, 70-4, 131-2, 150-3, 156, 170-1, 175
Shakespeare, William, 24, 43-5
  Plays cited, 31-3, 39, 43
Shannon, Edgar Finley, Junior, 117n., 137n., 168n.
Shelley, Mary, 57
Shelley, Percy Bysshe, 30, 57, 82, 94-110, 116, 117, 120, 121, 137, 138, 139, 145, 166, 173
  Adonais, 46, 97-110, 111, 122, 123 and n., 124, 135, 136

Shelley, Percy Bysshe (cont.)
  Epipsychidion, 95-6, 107
  Masque of Anarchy, The, 97
  Ode to a Skylark, 94-5, 97, 98
  Ode to the West Wind, 94, 97
  Prometheus Unbound, 15, 56-9, 97, 98
  Revolt of Islam, The, 98
  Sensitive Plant, The, 97, 98, 102
Sidney, Sir Philip, 102
Simile, see Imagery
Spenser, Edmund, 99
  Faerie Queene, The, 37, 87-9, 107
Spurgeon, Caroline F. E., 18n., 25
Stanford, W. B., 23, 25n., 27-8
Stevens, Wallace, 182
Svartengren, T. Hilding, 26n.
Swinburne, A. C., 168
Symons, Arthur, 24, 25, 179n.

Tate, Allen, 20n.
Tennyson, Alfred, Lord, 116-38, 139, 148, 149, 150, 153, 168, 176, 179
  Idylls of the King, The, 167
  In Memoriam, 42, 46-7, 116, 121-38, 145, 147, 149, 150, 153, 168
  Poems (1833), 117-18
  Poems (1842), 118-19
  Poems, Chiefly Lyrical, 116-17
Tennyson, Hallam, Lord, 122n.
Thomas, Dylan, 181n.
Thomson, James (B.V.),
  City of Dreadful Night, The, 169-79, 181
Thomson, J. A. K., 98n.

INDEX

Value-Words, *see* Vocabulary of Assertion
Virgil, 98n.
Vision of Love, *see* Love
Vocabulary of Assertion, 24, 48-50, 75-9, 80-1, 94, 109-10, 112-15, 137-8, 159-65, 178-9, 182
Voyage, The, as a poetic image, *see* Journey

Walker, Imogene B., 169n.
Warren, Robert Penn, 16n., 19n., 53n.
Wasserman, E. R., 52n.
Wells, H. W., 18n.

Wife of Usher's Well, The, 51
Willey, Basil, 135n.
Wimsatt, W. K., Junior, 12-14, 16-17, 19n., 22n., 35n.
Wordsworth, William, 15 and n., 46, 47-9, 56-79, 112, 116, 149, 153, 155, 166, 170, 176
  Prelude, The, 37, 42, 46, 48-9, 56-79, 80, 81, 84-5, 94, 111, 116, 150, 153, 165, 174n.
  Recluse, The, 56, 59
  Resolution and Independence, 34-5

Yeats, W. B., 11, 14, 15, 16, 24, 179, 181